The
North Wales
Castles Trail

20 splendid walks from castle to castle
through 235 miles of breathtaking scenery

The castles (or castle sites) are:
Chirk, Castell Dinas Bran, Caergwrle, Hawarden, Ewloe, Flint, Mold,
Ruthin, Denbigh, Bodelwyddan, Rhuddlan, Gwrych, Conwy,
Abergwyngregyn, Penrhyn, Beaumaris, Dolbadarn, Dolwyddelan,
Castell Tomen y Mur, Harlech, Criccieth & Caernarfon

Mike Stevens

Photography John Bell

KITTIWAKE

About the author

An experienced long-distance walker, Mike Stevens has lived in North Wales for over 30 years, where he has long been a champion of local walks linked to historical sites and trails. A well-known writer of plays based on local themes such as Gresford, The Mold Riots and By the Waters of Denbigh, all premiered in Mold's Theatr Clwyd, Mike Stevens is currently working on a new script set in North Wales at the time of the Armistice, 1918.

Dedication

I have been blessed over the years with many companions on my long walks. This book is partly a thankyou to them, to my son Dominic, Coast to Coast, to John and Rex Brayley, Offa's Dyke, Ian and Bridget McGarr, Phil and Heather Hodkinson, John French, Guy Britton, Terry Brown, and many pupils from Campion School, Bugbrooke who joined me on The Pennine Way, the Cleveland Way and Offa's Dyke, and to Hugh Taylor, the Pilgrim's Way and every step of the way finding the castles of North Wales.

This book is specially dedicated to my wife Suzanne, r companion on the Tour du Mont Blanc and on the tour itself.

Mike Stevens

Published by **Kittiwake Books Limited**
3 Glantwymyn Village Workshops, Glantwymyn, Machynlletl
Montgomeryshire SY20 8LY

© Text & map research: Mike Stevens 2018

© Maps: Kittiwake Books Limited 2018

© Photography: John Bell 2018

Care has been taken to be accurate.
However neither the author nor the publisher can accept responsibility for any errors which may appear, or their consequences.
If you are in any doubt about access, check before you proceed.

Printed by Mixam UK.

ISBN: 978 1 908748 56 0

Contents

INTRODUCTION

North Wales

I imagine you all know what we mean by 'North Wales', but in terms of castles I have drawn a line, perhaps harshly in some cases, with the southernmost fortification in the west being Harlech, and in the east Chirk.This has meant excluding Powis Castle ('one of the glories of Wales', writes Gerald Morgan) on the one hand and the fascinating outpost of Castell y Bere in the west. I also gave myself a headache trying to construct a journey to take in one castle after another. Even then it proved too difficult to do this without going back on myself, as you will see from the problem of including Beaumaris as part of a linear journey. I copped out by making two separate journeys from Penrhyn. Apart from that, this book provides a circular, anti-clockwise route of the remaining castles and sites in the region from CHIRK to CAERNARFON.

When is a castle a castle?

Before I started out devising the route, it hadn't occurred to me that perhaps I should have further defined 'castle'. You will find on your journey not only the archetype castle as built by Edward I, Rhuddlan, for example, but also bumps in the ground where there was a castle once, though sadly no more. Some of the original castles were built of timber, Mold for example, and inevitably all that remains now is the mound it was built on. But this is not a book about the history of castles. It is a guidebook of how to walk from one castle to another in a single day. In any case I do not have the authority of Gerald Morgan or Wynford Vaughan Thomas, so I hope you will turn to them and others for more exhaustive details about the castles mentioned. However it is probably a good idea at this stage to give a very quick overview of the chronology, and range, of the various places you will encounter on the trail. For some of the buildings it has been a case of gradual decline, Dinas Bran for example, now a splendid hill-top ruin. Others have gradually fallen down in out of the way spaces, like Ewloe, yet preserving a mysterious charm. Then there are the archetypal castles built by Edward I, as part of his 'Ring of Iron', Conwy, Flint, Beaumaris, Denbigh, Rhuddlan standing out on the landscape defiantly defying the ravages of time. Some have managed continually to reinvent themselves, like Chirk, which remains inhabited today. There are castles built by the Welsh princes, by the Norman invaders and even one built by the Romans. During the English Civil War several of the castles found themselves useful again, being occupied and defended by the Royalists or stormed and then slighted by the Parliamentarians. There are Victorian 'castles' as well, built for a new generation of 'princes', Penrhyn, Gwrych, Bodelwyddan. A whole host of fantastic sights for you to explore on the trail.

Type	Dates	Examples
* Neolithic/Iron Age hillforts	c 600 BC	Dinas Bran
* The Roman occupation	43–410 CE	Castell Tomen-y-mur
The Norman Conquest	11th Century	Mold
The Rise of Wales and the Welsh Princes	13th Century	Dolwyddelan, Criccieth
The English invasion of Edward I	13th Century	Flint, Conwy, Rhuddlan, Beaumaris
Assorted English kings, of the Plantagenet and Tudor variety	14th Century	Chirk
The Civil War re-occupation	1642-1651	Denbigh re-occupied by Charles I
New building for coastal defence	18th Century	1775 Fort Belan, near Caernarfon
Modernish	19th Century	Gwrych, 1819, Penrhyn 1822-1837, Bodelwyddan 1830-1832

See Gerald Morgan (2008) Castles in Wales, Y Lolfa.. *Wynford Vaughan Thomas (1973) The Splendour Falls, HTV Cymru * Terry Breverton (2010) Wales' 1000 Best Heritage Sites, Amberley*

Walking the walk

The complete trail

There are 20 walks in this book, each manageable in a day, with 15 miles being the optimum distance. You might want to run some of them together, Hawarden, Ewloe, Flint, for example make a good combination, or pick and mix, depending when and where you are in the area. There is no necessity to do them in any particular order. This trail, by the way, is of my own devising and is not a recognised national footpath, although it covers some ground already well-defined by long-distance walks such as Offa's Dyke, the Wales Coast Path, the North Wales Path and others.

A day's walking

It is possible to walk from one castle to another in a single day with strategic planning. To begin with, as with all linear walks, you need to plan your return to base at the end of the day. Probably the best way to do this is to make the destination castle your base, leave your car there and catch a bus, or train to the starting castle. Then use this guidebook to help you walk back to the car. You can use two cars, leaving one at your destination before travelling to your starting point in the other. Another way is to make the starting point your base and then catch the bus or train back after your day's walk. The problem is that you are then at the mercy of the clock, as we found trying to get back to Dolwyddelan from Trawsfynydd, and also the weather, including daylight..You may want to complete a couple of days' walking with accommodation in between, and as most of the castles are in towns, that is certainly possible. Even in Snowdonia the castles are quite close to centres of population, B & Bs and hostels.

Access to the castles

Some castles are open to the winds, Caergwrle for example, and are always accessible. Some have limited access and may require an entrance fee. Check before you start. One thing to bear in mind is that it is difficult to go round two castles in the same day, and also complete the walk in between. For example if you are based in Criccieth and take the train to Harlech, you may be restricted by opening hours of both castles, particularly as you have to walk back to Criccieth as well, and may run out of daylight, let alone opening hours, as happened to us on this stretch. One castle at least, Hawarden, is privately owned and difficult to access. You may have to settle for 'seeing' both castles rather than 'seeing around' them, or visit them on another occasion when there is more time at your disposal.

Footpaths

All the walks follow accepted footpaths and public rights of way, with some notable exceptions. The National Trust, for example, owns and manages some of the sites, and they have their own rules..You will see that I bring you only to the entrance of Penrhyn Castle. Similarly Chirk Castle can be approached only on a 'permissive' path, which is closed during winter months (I have provided an alternative here). Hawarden Castle can be approached via parkland, but is rarely open to visitors. Another problem is that to walk from one castle to another sometimes involves the use of roads. I have tried to avoid this wherever possible, but in order to approach Conwy Castle you have to negotiate the urban sprawl of Llandudno Junction. But there are worse sections. Although I used the footpath from Dolwyddelan Castle to Blaenau Ffestiniog on my way to Castell Tomen y Mur, a path which exists on the map, I would not recommend it and have not included it in this book, as the path is nowhere to be seen on the ground and is certainly not signposted. The alternative here is to walk by road over the Crimea Pass, a dismal prospect. It might be better to take a bus, or train. for the section from Dolwyddelan to Blaenau Ffestiniog and start the real walking there. The 5 mile length of road up the Llanberis Pass is also a killer, and unless you are a purist I would recommend catching the bus from Llanberis to Pen y Pass and picking up the walk to Dolwyddelan from there. The alternative, which you might prefer, incidentally, is to walk up Snowdon from Llanberis to Pen y Pass. It's certainly a good opportunity to climb Snowdon, which stands between the two mountain castles. I have included this alternative in the book. Perhaps it is also worth pointing out two other variations to footpaths on the trail. The first is a long stretch of cycleway on the way to Caernarfon, though I'm not sure how you could use your bike on other sections. The other is a bracing holidaymakers' stroll along the promenade from Rhyl to Abergele!

Terrain

It's hard to generalise about the going underfoot. I would imagine if you are choosing this sort of a walk, you will already be well equipped with a good pair of boots. Certainly in Snowdonia you will be traversing rough ground, and need to be well prepared. But even a stretch of gentle walking along pleasant country lanes can suddenly turn into a soggy trudge. There is one stretch out of Criccieth where you need to negotiate an inhospitable marsh. Even the most innocent-looking field can be ankle-deep in mud. Forest floors sprout roots to trip over, there are fast-flowing streams to cross, and featureless moorland may prove ankle-twisting territory. I have given a one-word description for the terrain to be expected over each walk, but that is a generalisation. I don't want to teach grandmothers to suck eggs, and I expect you are probably very experienced walkers to take on a trail like this, but spare a thought while you look at the view also to look where you put your feet.

Gradient

This trail takes you through some rough country, as you might expect of North Wales. Although some of the castles are on the coast, Flint, Conwy, Criccieth for example, land can rise quite steeply as you move inland. Once you reach Snowdonia, inevitably, gradients can be sharp, and severe. As well as anticipating the sheer steepness of the climb, do be prepared for the effect a gradient can have on speed. What may seem to be a short distance on the map, can take much longer to cover when climbing. I have given rough indications of the gradient for each section, but, once again, averaging may not tell the whole story.

Finding your way

Unlike most long-distance trails, this one, being newly invented, is not signposted as such. There are numerous waymarks, fingerposts, and direction indicators, but expect to find yourself sometimes on the Offa' Dyke Path, or the North Wales Path, or the Wales Coast Path or one of the others. Named pathways like this are usually well signed. On the other hand some local footpaths are poorly signed, perhaps reflecting the current shortage of money in the coffers of local authorities. I had to abandon one footpath which was indicated to cross the dual carriageway, the notorious A55, with a simple warning to 'take care'. The footpath was unusable, lethal in fact, so you will not find it in this book. Sometimes paths on the map are not the same as paths in real life, and in any case they may just give a rough indication of where you need to go. Do not always expect a 'path' to be easily spotted on the ground. I hope my notes will help.

Travelling to and from

On the whole bus services in North Wales, though infrequent, proved reliable when put to the test, particularly when having to change buses in the evening. Traveline Cymru is an excellent site to visit in order to clinch times and connections. The train also proved useful in some cases. Chirk is well served by the railway, but Caernarfon is not. We found trains from Flint to Hawarden and Criccieth to Harlech very handy. It is worth checking early on the times and frequency of public transport, as this can have an impact on your walking time, particularly if you are journeying in winter and have less daylight. The memory of trying to reach Denbigh Castle in the twilight is still with me.

You are in Wales

The first time you see the words 'Llwybr cyhoeddus' on a finger post, you may be thinking 'Do I want to go there?' until you realise that is the Welsh for 'Public footpath'. Wales is a bi-lingual country, and you will have no difficulty being understood, if you ask the way in English. As a matter of courtesy it helps to be able to say a few words in Welsh, even if only 'Bore da' and 'Diolch yn fawr'. Welsh place names and geographical features can sometimes give you an idea of what to expect en route, but you will soon distinguish between your 'Afon' and your 'Nant'. A list of commonly encountered Welsh words is included at the end of this section.

Equipment

If this is your first experience of long-distance walking, here are some suggestions. Old hands may well want to skip this paragraph. I can't emphasise enough the importance of good footgear. Trainers will be fine along the prom, but once you reach open country you will be glad of a good pair of boots. There are mountains involved on this trail, NO rock climbing it is true, but clambering over rocks, fording streams, negotiating featureless moorland and even working your way through muddy fields all require footgear up to the job. Be prepared for rain. This trail passes through Blaenau Ffestiniog, one of the wettest areas in North Wales, so a good anorak/cagoule will come in handy. It can be very cold, even in summer. When we climbed Snowdon in August, as part of this walk, the temperature at the top was barely 5°. And if you take to the hills during the winter months, hat, scarf and gloves are a necessity. Sometimes you can start a walk in pleasant sunshine, but find that you feel much colder as you climb. Be prepared. On the other hand it may be blisteringly hot, so take sunscreen, sunglasses and a sunhat. After all you may well be out in the sun for 8 or 9 hours, often when the sun is at its most intense. Mist can be a problem. Suddenly your sense of direction is affected as features disappear and you begin to lose your way. A compass is useful, and knowing how to use one is essential. Although the maps in this book will give you a very good guide, having a relevant OS Map with you to provide grid references and help compass work is a bonus. Maps will also give you a clear picture of your location measured against your surroundings. You should get into the habit of always knowing where you are on the map at any one time. I hear people say 'The map must be wrong' – and I've said it myself, but very often it's you who are wrong. In your rucksack (already full with everything I've mentioned so far) do make space for plenty of water and a packed lunch. On some of the walks you will never pass a shop. You also need a plan for emergencies. The mobile phone has made life much easier for walkers, and if something happens in Connah's Quay you will always be able to phone for help. Not so in Snowdonia, where there may not be a signal. If something happens out of the ordinary – sunstroke, for example, or a twisted ankle (and both of these have happened to me) you need to have a way of coping until help reaches you. So warm clothing, even a space blanket, will help until you can be reached. A whistle may seem over the top, but you may need to be able to draw attention to yourself, particularly if you walk alone. So it helps to have a companion. The unforeseen happens, and nature can be an unforgiving host if it does. Another thing: you're not being weedy to call off a walk even before you start, and if the weather forecast suggests heavy rain, low cloud or fierce winds, you might well be advised to postpone it until another day. Mountain rescue teams can provide many instances of walkers who were ill-prepared for their walk or went out in extreme conditions. *You are walking for the pleasure of it, after all.*

Some Welsh words you may encounter

Afon	river		Llan	church, village
Bryn	hill		Mynydd	mountain
Caer	wall, castle		Maes	field
Coed	wood		Newydd	new
Cwm	valley		Ogof	cave
Croes	cross		Pen	head
Dyffryn	valley		Pwll	pool
Eglwys	church		Pont	bridge
Ffrwd	stream		Rhaeadr	waterfall
Gwlad	land		Siop	shop
Hafod	summer dwelling, farm		Tyddyn	small farm, holding
Lôn	lane		Uchaf	upper
Llwybr	track, path		Ystrad	vale
Llyn	lake		Ystryd	street

1 CHIRK CASTLE to CASTELL DINAS BRAN, LLANGOLLEN

Chirk Castle

Resplendent in parkland and now owned by the National Trust, though with the family still in residence, Chirk Castle was originally built by Roger Mortimer in the 1290s, and had a chequered, though relatively undamaged, career.

11

Through peaceful fields then on to walk high above the glorious Vale of Llangollen.

Distance: 7 miles
Gradient: Mostly level, one steep climb
Terrain: Paths and fields and minor roads
Rating: Easy

* The footpath from Chirk goes past the castle along a public right of way. However the footpath taking you on from the castle is a permissive path, not a public right of way, and is only open from 1st April to 30th September. This does mean that during the winter months you need an alternative route from Chirk, given at † below.

* If you want to go round any of the castles en route, note that some are free to enter at any time (for example Castell Dinas Bran), some charge entry and/or have set hours of opening (Chirk, for instance). Some castles have even more restrictive access. See notes in the introduction.

* If you want to use public transport for this leg of this journey, there is a good bus service from Llangollen to Chirk, changing at Acrefair.

| From the centre of Chirk, take the road down towards the station. Once over the railway line and the canal, look out for a footpath to the right which will help you steer clear of the main road. (*The alternative path starts here. See † below*) This delightful path under trees will take you to a gate/stile on the left enabling you

to cross a field back up to the minor road. Turn right and almost immediately look out for the *permissive path* off to the left beside a bungalow. Go through a gate to follow a well-marked track, guided by white markers on posts. When you come to a junction of three fields, go through a kissing gate and bear left. With a fence on the left you will reach another kissing gate between a blue post and a white post. You now get your first view of the castle on your left. Continue to another gate which leads on to the approach road. Follow this approach road towards the car park and a junction, where you keep right as if to the car park. On the left is a small building where you can buy tickets for the castle. If you want to tour the castle this is the place to start.

2 To continue the walk after your tour of the castle, carry on along the roadway past the car park on your right to reach a new five-barred gate. *Note this is where the permissive path continues.* Go through and continue along the track with the fence on your left. After another field gate with a kissing gate by the side, forge ahead on the track. Another spanking new five-barred gate, also with a kissing gate by the side, allows you into a field and further on another gate takes you onto a road. Go left to the bend, then follow the road uphill. *The alternative path joins here. Move on to 3.*

† To follow the alternative path, leave Chirk as described, but when you come to the right-hand footpath, continue ahead along the road, making for the castle gates. Follow the tarmac road, left, as if to

the caravan park. At the entrance to the caravan park leave the road as it swerves left, and pick up a footpath. This footpath arrives at a T-junction. Take the right-hand one and plunge down through ancient woodland, with bluebells underfoot, and the castle grounds on the right. This brings you down to the Ceiriog Valley and the main B4500 road. Cross to the pavement on the other side and turn right. You run out of pavement and need to continue along the road chancing your arm (*and leg*) with traffic. Though a B road, it is deceptively busy, with some sharp bends. It is a good idea to stop when you hear traffic approaching and move onto the verge. The river runs swiftly to your left and you go past a trout farm (*a heron flew up as I passed*). You reach habitation and join the Offa's Dyke footpath. Here you turn sharp right, off the main road (thankfully) up a tarmac path. At a junction a waymark directs you onwards towards a white house, which you keep on your left,

mounting steadily upwards. Good views to your left of the Ceiriog Valley. The tarmac ends at the last habitation and you carry on upwards on a stony path. On a bend look out for a footpath going off to the right, well signed. Go through a kissing-gate into a field and continue steadily upwards towards the horizon. Behold a gateway. Go through to the brow of the hill. The paths appear to divide, *and I made the mistake first of going right. Don't do that.* Bear leftish, downhill. You are looking for a kissing gate in a fence which cuts right across your track, *guarded, in my case, by cows with huge horns and, wait for it, a bull no less. All perfectly peaceful. They will have moved on before you come along, I'm sure.* Go through the kissing gate into the field beyond. Aim for a splendid oak tree on the way to habitation. Beyond a redundant stile you reach a stony path, keeping the house to your right. You reach a kissing gate, and beyond that a road, where you turn left. *You have now completed the alternative route. Move on to point 3 now.*

3 Your route now is straight ahead, and upwards, on the minor road with some steep climbing. You reach a junction of paths. Take the sharp turn right and continue uphill on the road. You now join the Ceiriog Trail – a sign on the electricity pole confirms this, and you continue ever upwards on the road.

4 The road passes first through trees then opens out, giving wonderful views over to the right, including Beeston Castle and the Peckforton Hills in England. You reach a crossroads, and continue straight on, now on the brow of the hill, starting your descent. When you reach a T-junction, this is the signal for the end of road-walking and the start of the high spot of the walk as you follow the heights above the superb Vale of Llangollen. Go through the gate onto a by-way. On the far side of the valley, look out for the marked lines of escarpment, and beyond, if visibility is good, the Clwydian Hills, as they sweep onwards. Ignore the path off to the right and continue downhill now, through a gate across the path, with land falling steeply from left to right. Another field gate crosses your path. Continue steeply downhill, with excellent views of your next objective, Castell Dinas Bran, and look out for a parting of the ways, as the Ceiriog Trail leaves, off left, while we continue downhill.

5 A very steep descent on a stony path takes you to a gate, and beyond that a shrine, 'Ron's Roses' by the side of a minor road. Continue ahead along this minor road, past Tyn Dwr, looking out for a footpath, somewhat cunningly hidden on the left, marked, unsurprisingly, 'Llangollen'. Leave the road and follow this footpath uphill, steeply through woodland to a gate, round it and upwards through the wood, still steep. After a kissing gate the path descends to a fork, where you go downhill. Cross over two stiles to a section where the path opens out in a copse-like area. Ignore the immediate kissing-gate on the left and continue downhill to another kissing gate, and, once through, begin to see signs of habitation. You leave the footpath and reach a narrow tarmac road, where you turn left. This road takes you down into Llangollen. You may want to take in Castell Dinas Bran on your next walk, but if you want to climb up to the castle today, and it's quite a climb, read on.

2 CASTELL DINAS BRAN, LLANGOLLEN to CAERGWRLE CASTLE

This is the first of a few walks on this trail which are more than 15 miles in one day's march. So make an early start and enjoy the wonderful walk from Llangollen to World's End, the remote grouse moors of Esclusham mountain and the fertile valleys beyond. If doing this walk in a day, park your car in Caergwrle and catch an early morning train to Wrexham Central, and from there take a bus to Llangollen.

Distance: 16 miles
Gradient: Hilly, with some steep climbs
Terrain: Mixed, including featureless moorland
Rating: Strenuous

I An early challenge is the steep climb up to Castell Dinas Bran. Leave Llangollen town centre over the attractive Dee Bridge, and cross the road to the Taxidermy shop, (*that's right, Taxidermy*) and begin the ascent up Wharf Hill. Cross over the canal, past the first (and last) Tea room of the day, leaving the road to pick up a footpath opposite, signed 'Castell Dinas Bran', the school to your left. The familiar silhouette of the castle commands the skyline to your right. The footpath comes out through a kissing gate, crosses a track and continues on the steps uphill to another kissing gate.

Castell Dinas Bran

Towering above the Llangollen valley, a Welsh castle stood here from as early as 1073, this one built by Gruffudd ap Madog who died in 1209, the last occupant probably being Glyndŵr in 1402.

Cross a track to find a kissing gate guarded by (sculptured) ravens. There's only one way now, and it's uphill. Wonderful views emerge, the mysterious castle calling, reached by a series of staggered walkways. Wander across the close-cropped turf, peer through arches, marvel at old walls still standing on this windswept summit, and take in stunning views all round, but there's a long walk ahead, so make your descent.

2 Find the route downhill on the other side, making, it may seem, as if you're stepping off the edge of a cliff, but there are guided steps leading you towards the striking escarpment of Trevor Rocks on the far side. You may seem to be heading for the River Dee as it continues out of Llangollen. Find a grassy slope down to a more recognizable track and a black gate. The steep descent continues down steps and a grassy slope through gorse to join a road which emerges on your right-hand

15

side. Go through a kissing gate and turn left, following the road up to a T-junction, where you turn left again, following Offa's Dyke Path along a signed road.

3 After a mile or more you are joined by another road coming in from the left. Continue ahead, ignoring footpath signs off to the left and right as you go, but look out for a kind offering of water for thirsty travellers. The road negotiates a slight hill and dips down the other side, by the side of a coppice. The footpath takes its own route, off to the right, to carve its way along the steep edge of the escarpment, ascending slightly as you go. A dramatic stretch of walk, this.

4 Obey the prominent sign directing you downwards to the left, as you do have to descend, with the valley coming in from the left to meet you, as it were. Go through a kissing gate into a coppice. The half-timbered house over to the left is World's End Farm. Pass through a gate, and reach the head of the valley. After one more kissing gate the footpath comes out onto a road. Turn right and follow the road as it winds its way to ford a broad stream. Fortunately there are stout stepping stones for the pedestrian, but not all as stout as they seem. *One or two are quite wobbly.* You now have a long and rather steep walk up the road for a mile or more, much frequented by speeding cyclists, (*look out behind you*) and climb to the top of the hill.

5 Carry on along this road beyond the point where Offa's Dyke leaves abruptly, left, on its way to Llandegla, and follow the road down to the dip, where you will discover a prominent walkers' sign directing you off, left, into moorland. This is the last prominent sign for a while, so make the most of it, as a point of reference. *You now enter what can only be described as a featureless expanse of* bracken, heather and bilberries, guarded by buzzards with anguished grouse flying up from under your feet. There is a path, but it is often difficult to follow, and it's not much helped by very low walkers' signs on posts about 1 foot from the ground. I suspect in misty weather, or driving rain, either of which you might encounter up here, these signs will be hard to spot, and easier to trip over.

6 So, set off from the road along the winding path which will gradually descend to a brook, Afon Sychnant. *Keep your wits about you, as you try to keep up with the circuitous route.* Descend to find the babbling brook, which you leap over and progress on the other side. You now follow the direction of the stream which flows on your right. *Not much of a path here, we found.* The next objective is a kind of crossroads of paths. *Full marks if you spot, or stumble over, a waymark on a short post in the ground.* You reach the crossroads of paths. A makeshift bridge services a track coming in from the right, *expertly negotiated by a gamekeeper on a vehicle when we were last here. Don't cross the stream and don't follow the tempting broad track off up to the left.* Instead find, if you can, traces of a path through marsh grass, to continue in the same

direction as before, the stream a constant, though more distant, companion on your right. *Expect to make slow progress here, as the next section is difficult.* The stream begins to pass between defined banks to right and left, and as you continue, keep to the stream's left-hand bank. *Brownie points for spotting low-flying walkers' signs in the ground.* You will find that it's best to keep to the higher ground on the stream's left bank, as Afon Sychnant inhabits a very wet and marshy course. Even so, boggy, swampy sections abound. You will eventually see a tree ahead. This may not seem a useful target, but it is the first tree for a while, and the 'path', if path you find, will go quite close to it. With a bit of luck the tree approaches, or, rather, you approach the tree. When you reach it you will see it's thick and bushy, as it grasps the side of the stream's left bank Close by there is a walker's sign, low down. Pass the tree, on your right, to reach the brow of a hillock and signs of habitation ahead. The path, quite clear now, descends through heather and bracken (*ankle-twisting territory*). You reach a sign on a (much taller) post and discover you are now being sent sharply left and uphill, consistent with the route on the map. *Your errant journey over the moor is almost over.*

B5430 **9**
Old Road

Ty Hir Farm **8**

Aber Sychnant **7**

Offa's Dyke Path **6**

5

Worlds End Farm

4

7 Climb upwards, past a blasted tree on the left, through a gully and over the other side to a footbridge. The marshy path continues upwards and enters lone fir territory, eventually shaking itself to the right and squirming its way northwards to reach a field boundary. Keep the field boundary on your right and continue through moorland edge to reach a gate and stile.

8 Here you leave the moor and proceed along a more recognisable track up towards the farm ahead, Ty Hir Farm. Go through the gate into proper farm territory (you may see a walkers sign on a post in front of you) and turn left into the farm yard, passing between sheds and barns to come out on the other side. Descend away from the farm on its access road. After passing another farm you will come down to a junction, where you pick up the yellow minor road, and turn right. Follow this straight road, or lane, all the way to the junction with the 'Old Road', the B5430, where you turn right. Go uphill along this main road, and shortly find a footpath going off to the left to enter a field.

in a field with no less than three stiles at exit points. Aim for the stile on the right, uphill, and cross this nice new piece of field furniture and continue along the level with the fence on your right. There is another stile in the fence on your right, which you cross, so that you now proceed with the fence on your left. A stile awaits you in the field corner. Cross over into a coppice and follow the path through bracken. You're on the edge of a quarry here, so take note of warning signs. You start to descend to a gate. In the next field, which slopes down from the right with gorse, keep close to the fence to your left. Here be goats. Leave the field in the corner through a gate and pass between houses onto a driveway.

Nant y Ffrith

B5101

⑬ Ffrith

⑫

⑪

A525 ⑩ Bwlchgwyn

9 Cross the stile (*Sign: Bwlch Gwyn ½ mile*) and once in the field keep close to the field edge on your right. *Beware loose barbed wire ahead.* You reach a stile in the field corner, cross and find yourself

10 Bear left, but look out for a cunningly hidden gunnell opposite the new houses taking you down past a graveyard, on your left, which brings you to the main road. Cross the main road with care and pick up the path on the other side, with a prominent walkers' sign leading you downhill. Cross the stile here (*big step down*) and descend the sloping field, which turns out to be two fields separated by a stile and perhaps a prancing horse in the second one. Descend to the field corner and a gate taking you onto a lane, where you turn right. Follow the road between houses. Look out for a lane left, which you need to reach before the continuation of the footpath. Go down this lane for a short distance to discover a walkers' sign in the hedge, on the right. *The direction on this sign is mysterious and possibly misleading.* So, once in the field, descend following the direction of the power lines, a sort of half-left direction

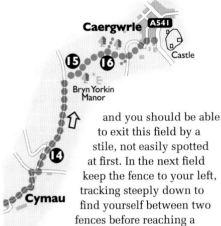

Caergwrle `A541`

Castle

⑮ ⑯

Bryn Yorkin Manor

⑭

Cymau

and you should be able to exit this field by a stile, not easily spotted at first. In the next field keep the fence to your left, tracking steeply down to find yourself between two fences before reaching a stile, steps and a footbridge bringing you out on a road, where you turn left. *Say goodbye to fields for a bit.*

11 Follow the road, steeply uphill to a farm, continuing round to cross a stream over a bridge and join another road where your turn right, and on towards the entrance to Nant-y-Ffrith. Just before you reach the gated entrance and information panel, look out for a bridleway, off to your right. Go through a gate and muddy gateway onto the path, with woodland edge on the left and hedgerow to the right and an ancient way with catkins and snowdrops (*in season*). The path starts to dip as you descend close to power lines becoming steeper, through pines. You now reach habitation on the right, as the bridle way joins a driveway. Turn left here by the growling brown bears (*only kidding*) and follow the drive away from the house.

12 The stream is close by, on the right, as it chortles its way to a bridge, which the drive crosses but you don't.

Instead, as the drive makes its way with a sharp right turn, continue upwards past rhododendrons. The path levels out at the top marked by a gate and a kissing gate. Paths join here, but your route is decidedly downhill towards Ffrith, as indicated by a walkers' sign on a post in the ground. Your descent here is straightforward, and now is a good time to step it out down this broad track. One section takes you between fences to circle a house, followed by a gate. Otherwise it's full steam ahead to Ffrith, under the old railway bridge, past the (*abandoned*) Bluebell Inn to reach the main road, where you turn left.

13 Go uphill on this main road (*it may not look main, but it carries a lot of traffic*), past the newly refurbished Poacher's Cottage to a road junction. This is an extremely dangerous junction, for a pedestrian, so I suggest you walk up the narrow road on the left hand side until you are almost at the signpost before crossing the road and taking the road, right, to Cymau (*also a bus route, so look out for the occasional large vehicle*). This is Cymau Lane and you continue along here, mindful of a footpath sign on a post, off left. Leave the road and go down steps into woodland, with a house on the left. Go uphill now, quite significantly, through scrubland, with primroses and celandines (in season), marked well by walkers' signs on posts. On your way up this steep path you reach a stile and beyond that another path joins you from the left. Continue, to the right, and now on the level, losing height a little with houses to right and left. You come to a junction of paths. Ignore the path to the right and carry on to the kissing gate, with a yellow walkers' sign on a post, and go through the gate onto an access road, tarmac, and here turn right.

14 After the house on the left, notice that a walkers' sign on a post seems to direct you, left, upwards. However, carry on along the road for a short distance taking a left-hand road where it forks. At the top you come to Stanfield House. Here you take the public footpath through the property to reach an ancient low stone stile which you easily cross and turn right. This is an official Wales Link Path, and it follows the field on your left on two sides. It keeps close to property on the right, but swings round steeply upwards, left to a stile and comes out on a road, where you turn right.

15 Follow the road for a short distance downhill until you reach a fork where you take the left-hand road. Uphill now, the road divides again, but this time take the right-hand fork, by-passing a house on the right, and continue slightly uphill. The valley floor opens up to your right. This pleasant minor road now decides to progress more steeply upwards. The sharp ascent up the road levels out a bit, and you are rewarded with good views over to the right as far as Beeston Castle and the Peckforton Hills. Continue along this road for a short distance, looking out for a footpath going off to the right. Caergwrle appears down to your right and you may get glimpses of the castle, though it is somewhat dwarfed by the high hill behind. On the right you reach the spanking new waymark on a post, (*Caergwrle ¾ mile*) a good stile and well-cared for steps into the field. Another sign low down on a post seems to suggest a more leftish route, but ignore this and once over the stile descend sharply to a waymark on a post in the middle of the field. Take your bearings when you reach this midway post. Aim for the wood ahead along a distinct path in the field.

16 As you approach the wood you will see a stile and a waymark on a post, brand-new, and the final descent into Caergwrle. Once over in the woodland descend sharply over two stretches of duckboard. Down below, to your right, is Bryn Yorkin Manor. A slippery path winds its way steeply down to a gate. Once through here you meet an unusual warning sign: *CAUTION ARCHERY IN PROGRESS.* Fortunately you do not need to encounter Robin's Merry Men, as the footpath continues its descent, right, through woodland edge. This section is well-signed with posts in the ground, and you continue downhill to reach a broad path crossing your route. Here turn sharp left along the broad track for a very short distance and then almost immediately leave it as you plunge down, right, by a walkers' sign on a post. A steep, slippery and muddy section follows, and you come to a spot where the paths divide, marked by a wooden post in the ground with a blue marker on top. Go right here to a stile leading into a well-established apple orchard. Wind your way to find an exit stile enabling you to cross a tarmac road. There are more stiles and roads to cross as you, perhaps wearily, descend abruptly into Caergwrle. After the last stile you reach a steep narrow road, turn right and then left into the housing estate. You reach a footpath sign on a post, allowing you to turn right between houses. This tarmac footpath brings you out onto the main main road where you turn left along the pavement into Caergwrle. To reach the castle cross this main road before the dangerous left-hand bend. Just past the war memorial you will see signs directing you upwards to the castle and your objective for the day.

3 CAERGWRLE CASTLE to HAWARDEN CASTLE

Caergwrle Castle

Built by Dafydd ap Gruffudd in 1277, this castle was seized and occupied by Edward I for himself and Queen Eleanor, the incomplete building being accidentally burnt down soon afterwards.

A gentle ramble along the ancient rampart Wat's Dyke to reach the parkland surrounding Hawarden Castle.

Distance: 8 miles
Gradient: Level
Terrain: Paths and fields
Rating: Easy

1 *If you are coming to Caergwrle by car, park in the free car park just off Mold Road.* Coming out of the car park, turn right and cross the road on the sharp bend by the 'Olde Castle Inn' to reach the war memorial. Then go to 3 below.

2 *Another useful way of reaching Caergwrle is to park your car at* Hawarden station and catch the train to complete the short journey to Caergwrle. From Caergwrle station, go down the steps and ramp to the main road, the A550. *If you have already visited the castle and simply want to continue on the walk, turn right on the A550 and rejoin this guide at 4 below.* To visit the castle, however, after leaving the station turn left at the main road, cross and go under the railway bridge, turning sharp right immediately into Castle Street. This street has an intermittent pavement, so face oncoming traffic uphill, then switch to the other side. Continue along Castle Street until it joins the A 494 and follow the road round, left, to the war memorial.

3 From the War Memorial there is a good path winding uphill, rather steep in parts, with one good viewing bench, before you come to Caergwrle Castle on the top of the hill. After wandering about among the ruins descend back to the War Memorial the way you came. To choose an alternative way down, with your back to the castle take a route sloping through bracken, using the tower of Castle Cement on the horizon as a marker, and descend, until you come to a place where paths seem to go left and right. Turn left, follow the path down to the road at the bottom and turn right into Castle Street. Continue all the way down, changing to the left-hand side of the road on the sharp bend, to reach the busy A550, where you turn left and pass under the railway bridge.

4 Follow the A550 for a short distance, spanning the river Alyn. Cross the main road and turn right into a road marked Rhydyn Hill. You can cut the corner here to look more closely at the river, the weir, the mill, the bridge, all enhanced by European money (*remember Europe?*), with details on a plaque. Continue past the former Corn Mill to go up the steep tarmac of Rhydyn Hill. Look out for another information plaque on your right, which gives details of life in Caergwrle when it was a Spa Town (*oh yes it was!*) and also relics of its industrial past in the shape of a brewery and bottling factory. On the left-hand side of the road, after a short distance, look out for a footpath which will take you up from the road into woodland, by way of steps to a stile with waymark. You are now on the long distance trail, the Wat's Dyke Way. Continue uphill, with mesh fencing and houses on the right. When you come to another stile with a waymark, cross over into woodland edge. The pleasant path continues with an open field on the left,

between trees, and you start to go downhill. Pass a post on the left with a waymark. At the bottom you need to turn sharp right and walk up as if into the wood. But after going through a walkers' gate, turn sharp left immediately, to follow a path, fenced on both sides. The path turns sharp right, the fenced field still on your right. You are now on the ancient Wat's Dyke itself, although not really able to appreciate it, except by noticing the deep ditch over to the left. You come to another walkers' gate. The path now takes a sharp right turn uphill.

5 Go through another

walkers' gate to gain access onto the busy Gresford road and turn sharp left to follow the main road for a short distance, before turning left again into a one-way road. This will take you into the neighbouring village of Hope, bringing to mind the local saying, *'Live in Hope, Die in Caergwrle'*. The road takes you directly to the church, where you will see a walkers' sign on a post, directing you to the right. Follow this route back to the Gresford road, which you cross with care to gain the lane opposite, with a walkers' sign on a post. Follow this lane past the building on the left, looking out for a footpath also on the left. Sure enough there is a waymark on a post by the electricity pole, so leave the lane and descend to a stile and cross into a field where you turn half-right. *You may experience some difficulty in orientation at this point.*

6 Make for some trees. You will see a fence ahead, marking the edge of the field, and you aim to reach a point where this fence meets the trees. You are going uphill now, but not to the top of the hill. Keep the hilltop and gorse on your right before going down slightly to find a pathway by the side of the fence. You are now walking under trees before reaching a junction of fields, muddy in wet weather. There is a stile here, on your left. Cross and enter the field beyond. Once in the field bear right, going uphill close to the hedge on your right, power lines overhead, making for a stile.

7 Once over the stile, in the next field keep the hedge close on your right still, uphill, ignoring a field gate on the right, going straight on with a good view of Beeston Castle in Cheshire (*not that you're going there*). You come to the end of the hedge on your right to find a stile also on your right, by the side of the power line pole. Cross the stile. In the next field continue in the same direction as before with the fence now on your left. Follow the power lines and keep the open cornfield to your right. You will reach the field corner and a high hedge ahead. Turn sharp right here, following the edge of the cornfield.

The hedge is on your left now, the open cornfield on your right. You need to turn left before you reach the end of this field, so cross the stile by the side of a metal gate and pole, and now go straight ahead, making for another metal gate. *The day we walked, the field on the left had an electric fence and an inquisitive white horse.* At the side of the metal gate is a stile. Cross onto a grassy track to reach another gate, which you open, to find another grassy track with a high wooden fence on your left. The track turns into a driveway and you come out on a minor road, where you turn left.

8 *There follows a stint of road walking now, but there is little traffic, although the road is narrow and you might find farm machinery creeping up as you progress.* Follow the road to Shordley Manor and a slightly staggered crossroads. Go across and continue along the road ahead, past a house called The Stocks and look out for a bridleway on your right. At first this is a definite road, but when this turns sharp right continue ahead along the bridle path which becomes much more of a lane, marked by a prominent stone. Continue along this delightful lane, descending eventually as you turn sharp left under a beautiful beech tree, and continue, slightly uphill, along the lane, eventually becoming metalled as you join houses. This lane turns into a proper road. Continue uphill to reach a road junction and turn right.

9 This is more of a major road, but walk only as far as a bridge where you need to look out for a footpath going off and upwards to the left. Go through a walkers' gate where you are faced by a slope. You cannot be sure of your direction here, but climb the slope until features become clearer. Once on top, look ahead for a building with a red roof, which is in fact a pair of semi-detached houses. Head for the houses and on your way through the fallow

23

field you will reach a field gate. Go through here and aim now for the tree to the right of the houses with the red roofs. Beyond this splendid but careworn oak tree you will find a walkers' gate which will take you out onto a road, where you turn right.

10 More road-walking ahead on a minor road (*with little traffic*) called Bramley Lane, flush with rose bay willow herb and meadowsweet on our last visit. Pass Bramley Farm on your left and look out for a footpath on your left, marked by a sign, and use the walkers' gate to gain access into a field (with cows, perhaps) Keep close to the hedge on the left hand side until you reach the field corner, where there is a walkers' gate and beyond that a duck pond, complete with ducks. Keep the pond on your right and make for the field corner and a final walkers' gate before reaching a field gate which takes you onto a road, where you turn right at Bramley Hall Farm. Follow this minor road to a much busier road, Kinnerton Lane, where you turn left. Keep a sharp eye out for traffic here as you continue along Kinnerton Lane up to a T-junction, where you turn right onto the hostile A5104, bristling with traffic. *This formidable road needs to be mastered with care.* Battle your way along the roadside, but only for a short distance you will be pleased to hear.

11 After this short downward march, look out for an open gateway on the left. There is no sign here, but this is the footpath, or cart track rather, taking you through first one field and then another. The track keeps close to the hedge in the first field, but in the second, garlanded with poppies and feverfew, goes straight across towards trees and the ferocious A55. *Fortunately you do not have to negotiate this trunk road because you are looking for a secret tunnel.* Once across the field you will come to a field gate and a stile, and

at once catch sight of the well constructed (*but not much used, I suspect*) tunnel. Enter.

12 Once you emerge on the other side, follow the overgrown path between houses to come out onto a road where you turn right. Follow this access road for a while until you see a walkers' sign on a post on the left-hand side, and exchange one road for another, Cherry Orchard Road. This proceeds in a straight direction gradually becoming less metalled until it eventually mutates into a lane and finally into a path as it enters Bilberry Wood. You now enter privately owned woodland, although there is a public right of way through it. The official "footpath" through

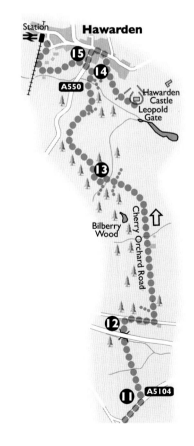

the wood soon turns sharp left and then immediately sharp right. Continue through the wood.

13 The path veers right and left and slightly uphill. You will eventually make your way through pleasant woodland, over a stile to reach a wall. Walk on with the wall on your right-hand side and a field over to the left. The path dips into a ditch on the left, past a redundant stile with a waymark on it and descends through old woodland on a very broad path with a stream first on your left, then on your right. You come to a gate, a stile and a broad path, continuing through woodland, crossing over a broader stream, red with iron ore, passing an old mill on the right. As you descend you are now beginning to leave the wood, and climb up into a car park.

14 To reach the castle from here, walk up along the pavement from the Car Park to the main road and turn right to face the imposing entrance to Hawarden Castle. *There is an information board which says that the public is welcome to walk in the grounds 'most days of the year'. Before you set off though, you need to know you are going to be walking in park grounds, and will only be able to reach the wall surrounding the castle, and not the castle itself, except when it is open to the public on selected days in the Spring and Summer months (such as August 12th 2018).* So, if the main gate is open, go through the gate within a gate and a short stretch will take you to a further gate across the tarmac footpath. You are now in parkland. Follow the easily identified tarmac footpath, until it ends in a traditional five-barred gate. Just before you reach the gate you will find a path, left, going up hill, under lime trees. Now you will catch glimpses of the castle beyond the wall as you reach Leopold Gate, with dates and timings of admission. *Pay and go through into the castle grounds, if it's your lucky day.* Most interesting is the round tower, with its several levels, reached by steps. The inner courtyard, almost amphitheatre-like, houses the Great Hall, whose upper window arches remain. Once you have feasted on the castle remains, or if it is not your lucky day from Leopold Gate, retrace your steps back to the main entrance.

15 *Now in Hawarden you may need to retrieve your car which you left at the Station.* There is an attractive walk from the Car Park you reached earlier. Cross, and go down the main road facing you, the A550, for a short distance, looking for a footpath off to the right. Go over the stile here and down into countryside, with the golf course on the left and woodland edge to the right. You come to another stile at this point. Keep the golf, the pool and the geese on your left, walking along on the level. At the end of the footpath you come to a gate. You now enter some kind of a yard, *perhaps with moving machinery.* Go out of the yard into an access drive, turn sharp right and uphill. At the top you are in a housing estate, turn sharp left into Woodlands Court, go down to the station to be re-united with your waiting car.

4 HAWARDEN CASTLE to EWLOE CASTLE en route for FLINT CASTLE

Hawarden Castle

Built on an Iron Age site, now owned and occupied next door by the Gladstone family, the Norman castle was developed by Llywelyn, and figured in the dispute between the two Welsh princes before falling into English hands in 1283

Two castles in one journey: the hidden woodland mystery of Ewloe, before you reach the gaunt ruin of Flint Castle beside the estuary of the River Dee.

Distance: 8 miles (2½ miles Hawarden to Ewloe, 5½ miles Ewloe to Flint)
Gradient: Mostly level
Terrain: Paths, fields and roads, through some built-up areas.
Rating: Moderate

I A This is the route from Hawarden Station. Leave Hawarden station car park and go uphill to the main road, the B5125, cross the road and turn right in the direction of the village of Hawarden. Walk along the pavement to find a footpath, well marked, off to the left, opposite the 'Shared Olive' restaurant. Now walk downhill along the footpath, with a high grassy hill on the left and a high fence on the right. You pass between houses and come out onto a main road, the A550, where you turn left. The high hill is in fact the site of an early Motte and Bailey castle, undefined. Follow the pavement downhill. Just before the road coming from the right, Cross Tree Lane, look out for a footpath going off to the left. *Here this stage of the walk joins the walk from Hawarden Castle. Go to No 2.*

1B *If you are walking from Hawarden itself, directions from the imposing entrance to Hawarden castle are as follows.* Cross the main road carefully to the pub opposite, the Glynne Arms, and turn left. Cross Rectory Road and continue along the pavement past the Post Office until you reach a road going off to the right, marked Gladstone Library and walk down to the archway of Church Gates. Enter the churchyard, where there is a good ground plan. Walk as if to the church, enter if you wish or go round the building to find a tarmac path continuing downhill under impressive yew trees, past a sign indicating 'Crimean War grave' until this tarmac path divides three ways. Take the lefthand path towards the lych gate, and from there down steps to a path onto the main road, the A550. Cross the busy road and continue downhill, looking for a footpath signed off to the left. *Read on.*

2 A walkers' sign on a post takes you off the main road here and into more open country. Not far along this walkway you come to a walkers' gate. Go through the gate and cross a field, maintaining height and aiming for a pylon which you can see in the middle distance. At the end of the field, go through a gap in the hedge, noticing an overgrown and redundant stile on your right. Cross the next field towards a hedgerow and a walkers' gate. Go through this kissing gate and continue in the same direction, with a hedge close by on your left and a more substantial field on the right,

sloping away, *perhaps with cows.* You reach another kissing gate in the corner to pass through into scrubland with property on the right.

3 Keep close to the high boundary fence on your right along a good path. Invisible over to the left is the railway line from Bidston to Wrexham. Descend by steps onto a road. To the left, straddling the road, is the arch of a high railway bridge. Cross the road to find a footpath opposite, shown by a walkers' sign on a post. Follow the path with houses on the right. You are now entering a new housing estate *which does not figure on the current OS map.* Carry on between houses by road as it curves right with a play area on the left. *Ignore the temptation to play*, and continue downhill for a short distance to discover a tarmac path going off to the left. Leave the road and follow the path to a kissing gate. The walkers' sign here shows you need to cross the next field half right. Keep the hedge on your right to the field corner. Here ignore the footpath off to the right, but use a gate to gain access onto a road, bearing right. You follow this (yellow) minor road as it goes slightly downhill and narrows, with buildings on both sides. As you go uphill slightly, look out for a footpath going off to the left. Sure enough there it is, under a road sign. Turn off the road here, by the side of a fairly imposing gated entrance and follow the footpath. The wall on the left gives way to a fence with property on the right as you continue along the footpath to the railway line. Cross the railway by the convenient tunnel underneath, and, once through, turn right. There is a footpath sign, but more of a guide for walkers going uphill. Your route is to turn right and follow the railway line close by on your right. *This leads to some complicated moves now, as you negotiate the next formidable obstacle, the thundering A494, known as 'Aston Hill'.*

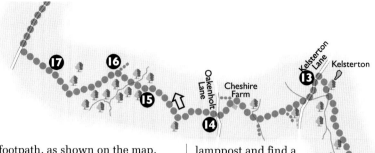

4 The footpath, as shown on the map, now takes you away from the railway line, crossing the field, half left. *But we discovered that if you continued along by the side of the railway line you would still reach your objective.** However, if you are following the footpath, cross the field, half left to reach a line of trees, turn right now keeping these trees on your left and make for the road. *Some standing water on this section.* You will reach a stile at the foot of the road embankment. Once over the stile go up to the ear-splitting roadside. You will be glad to know you do not have to cross the road, where you would face certain maiming, because you are being directed to a subway. *Ah, but where is it?* Go right, downhill, on a sort of pavement, some distance, to reach the railway line (again) as it passes underneath the road. This is where you would have come, if you had continued your earlier route*. Just after the bridge you will see you can leave the road to scramble down towards houses. Passing the houses on your right you come to a road, and looking left you will indeed see the subway. Go through the subway, up the other side and continue, uphill now, on the other side of the road, *which is not much different from the first experience, except the traffic is now pounding its way down, mostly ignoring the 50mph sign.* You are aiming to reach a point opposite the spot where you came up from the field. As you strive upwards against the noise, first of all cross a minor road coming in from the right, and carry on uphill to reach a high

lamppost and find a footpath taking you off to the right and away from the traffic. *Hooray! Back to the countryside.*

5 Descend the ramp to a stile. Once over, you will find two paths, one going uphill. Ignore this and take the other, half right through emerging woodland, slightly uphill, with a fence on the right Continue uphill (*this is the pedestrian version of Aston Hill after all*) as scrubland narrows to a corner and a gate by a walkers' sign. Go through the gate, and continue along the track, fenced left and right, to come out onto a tarmac access road. This is Church Lane, you will discover when you come to the end of it. You reach a minor road.

6 Cross the road and pick up a broad tarmac lane, signed as a footpath, to reach a point where the footpath divides, just below Aston Hill Farm on the map. Take the left-hand footpath, crossing a stile. Clip the field to reach a walkers' gate opposite. Go through the gate into a field. *Some orientation is needed here.* Enter the field with a pond in it. Keep the pond, which is encircled by shrubs, well over to the right and find, if you can, a path to traverse the field, leaving a deepening ditch to your left. You are walking parallel to power lines on your right. *Do not be* alarmed to discover you are now walking slightly north of Stockholm. Maintain height and avoid the land sloping away to the left. Make for an oak tree. As you approach the tree the path, if path there be, gives a shake, right, and goes uphill, with hedge on the left to reach a junction of power lines. Go under one stretch of power lines, turn sharp left and go under the next. Continue downhill aiming for habitation. A good view of Moel Fammau on the Clwydian Hills in the distance. The path follows the field round to the right and comes out onto a minor road, Shotton Lane. Cross by means of a stile into the lane and turn left. Follow Shotton Lane down to a T-junction and turn right onto the pavement by the side of the B5125, which you follow.

7 Look out for a walkers' sign on a post indicating a footpath off to the right. This will take you first of all to a (*still padlocked?*) field gate, which you have to climb to reach a field. You need to cross this field, going slightly up hill, keeping a muddy pond of sorts on your left, with a prominent house as a marker ahead and somewhat to the right. The real marker to aim for, though, is a large tree in the hedgerow on the far side of the field and left of the prominent house. By the side of the tree there is a stile, and a walkers' sign. You are now in another field which you need to cross. There is a gap in the hedge opposite and a kissing gate, very narrow, which brings you out onto a tarmac lane. Cross to the kissing gate opposite, and take the path going downhill. You are now in a Site of Special Scientific Interest and the splendid ancient woodland of Wepre Woods. As you descend along this broad track, look out for a secondary path off to the left which will take you down via steps to cross a stream, and up more steps to the fascinating Ewloe Castle, remote, mysterious and unlike most castles on this trail, hidden from sight.

EWLOE CASTLE to FLINT CASTLE

8 After exploring, climbing and lunching perhaps in the environs of Ewloe Castle, it's time to start the walk from here to the next castle at Flint. In some ways the most direct route from here would be to descend through the splendid Wepre Wood and Wepre Park to reach the road all the way down to Connah's Quay and pick up the Wales Coast Path. Unfortunately this is possibly the most tedious section of WCP, involving several miles of pavement bashing along the main coast road, not really a coast path at all until you reach the outskirts of Flint. So, take the more enjoyable rural inland route. There is one built-up section, but even this is pleasant enough.

Descend from Ewloe Castle on the north west side into

29

the deep gully via steps with a handrail to a footbridge over the two streams. Instead of taking the main path through the woods, look for a series of steps up on the left. Ascend the steep steps to the top of the gully, where you come out onto a field with a gate on the left. Go round the gate and tree, and turn right, following the path with a field on your left and a hedgerow immediately on your right. The path now dives under scrub willow, pleasantly overhanging, into another field. Continue in the same way until the path ends at a low level stile, which brings you out onto a road, which turns out to be Wepre Lane. Turn right and follow the road round to a junction. Cross the continuation of Wepre Lane to the pavement on the other side and begin your excursion through the housing estate.

9 You begin by following a short road, Melford Place, and take the next road left, Vaughan Way This will bring you to a road junction and a main road, Llwyn Drive, where you turn right opposite the Primary School. Walk along the pavement, and cross a road coming in from the right, which is Vaughan Way again. The road you are following opens out with an open green space on the left. Opposite the car park effect on the other side, there will appear a footpath on your side going off to the right, marked by a walkers' waymark pole, shorn of its sign. Follow the sturdy path between houses as it swings round left behind lock-up garages. Over to the right is more of an open space and the beginning of valley, but carry on along the tarmac, as it leaves the houses on the left and swings round to the right and you come to a local nature reserve known as Llwyni Pond. Go through the little gateway and the path veers to the right with good views of Shotton Steelworks to your right. At the end of this tarmac path turn sharp right, through the narrow gate and make as if for the steelworks, *which*

don't look at all like your vision of a steel works, by the way.

10 You now follow a tarmac path which will take you down through the steep ways between new houses. First of all you come to a road. Cross and continue down by the splendid rowan tree, bringing you down to a sort of court, serving several houses. Continue in the same pattern and another Court to another road, Devon Place. Continue downhill as before along this well-maintained path, a sign saying 'Circular Walk' and follow this gunnell to a junction of paths. The way off to the right through woods looks tempting, but is to be ignored. Instead turn left and continue along the tarmac path, high fence to the right and wall to the left. You now come out onto another road with pavements which you follow to join onto another road, Chiltern Close. Cross the road in front of you to continue along narrow tarmac passageway between houses. When you come out, turn left at house no 39 Bodnant Grove and go slightly uphill to reach a slip road which runs parallel to the main Mold Road. Turn left, making for a sign which says Cliveden Road and now make your way over to the Mold Road proper, over to your right. Cross the busy road when it's safe, and continue uphill climbing out of Connah's Quay. You run out of pavement and reach the brow of the hill. There is in fact a trig-point marker embedded in the wall on your right. Go under power lines and look for the Bridleway sign, off to the right. Your trek through the housing estate is complete.

11 The bridle way is tarmac at first, providing access to the houses on the left before giving way to a more foot-friendly surface. Continue along the bridle path until you reach a gate on your right-hand side. Go through the gate into a field. As you look across the field, you

Ewloe Castle

A Welsh castle, probably built by Llywelyn ap Gruffudd in the 13th century, this fortification was left to decline after Edward I's invasion, probably because it had little strategic value.

will see a similar gate in the hedgerow on the other side. When you reach this gate, however, turn left along the field edge to find a kissing gate, to the right-hand side and you are now in another field with a view of Connah's Quay Power Station over to the right, tempered by another view of the magnificence of the River Dee Estuary. Cross this fairly large field on the diagonal, going under power lines to find a large tree. Views over to the right continue with good sightings of the splendid Bridge over the Dee and beyond the river the sturdy high ground of England, the Wirral in fact. Just to the right of the tree is a kissing gate, taking you through into another field, the crop being maize on our last visit. Keep left here, with the hedge close on your left, thriving with rose bay willow herb and giant hogweed to come out through a muddy patch onto a road, where you turn right onto a tarmac road, Golftyn Lane. Continue down Golftyn Lane as it begins its steep descent into habitation, but keep a weather eye out for a footpath beyond a kissing gate with walkers' sign high up in the hedgerow to your left, yielding access into open country.

12 There now follows an exhilarating, enjoyable stretch of walking along the crest of a spur of land. Continue along this high spot, with good views ahead and to the right, making first for a gap between a tree and hedge. *Really fantastic views here of the Dee Estuary opening up and joining the Irish Sea. The tide may be up when you come, or you may have spectacular sighting of the broad expanse of the Sands of Dee.* Cross a stile, with a waymark and continue in the same direction, with the land falling away on both sides. You come to a field edge and begin your descent. This fascinating walk ends in a gate across your path *which looks like a climbing job, but no, this can be unhooked.* Follow the path down through a narrowing field, woodland over to the left, which you approach as you descend. Pass between a splendid pair of stone gateposts, without a gate, and you will eventually reach a pretty stream, which you need to cross. There is a wooden bridge, which is not much help, being overgrown, so go a bit further on and find an easier place to cross. On the other side you may have a hacking job through brambles and nettles to find a manageable path with the stream on the right, going under trees, old oaks probably part of Kelsterton Hall estate. Walk or wade through a marshy area, under trees on a recognisable path which broadens out and you come to the end at a stile in the corner. Turn left onto Kelsterton Lane.

13 Walk along the road, Kelsterton Lane, tarmac surface, bending, with sudden traffic, and look out for a walkers' sign on a post in the hedgerow to the right, leading into a short, broad area towards another stile. After this stile take just a short step in the field and turn left, following the boundary line of the property to your left. After you have passed the house, the actual path cuts directly across the field to a corner and stile which cannot be seen. *On our visit the field was resplendent with barley, and in deference to the farmer, we walked round two sides of the field to reach the stile.* So, after the first field edge, bear right and follow the second field edge to the (*possibly overgrown*) stile in the corner, now on your left. Once over the stile clip the next field half right to reach another stile in the hedgerow. In the next, somewhat larger, field you can see a giant power line mast ahead. The stile you want is just behind it, so head off for the mast and find the stile. A walkers' sign indicates a right turn, so once over the stile (*also overgrown, but it was July*) bear right, keeping the hedgerow to your right and make for Cheshire Farm. The path becomes a track and, as you go through a gate, turns into a recognizable access road to the farm. Traverse the farm yard, keeping Cheshire Farm on your left, and ignore the footpath tempting you to continue ahead, and instead turn left and follow the driveway to the road, which is in fact Oakenholt Lane.

14 *You may be thinking this is a good point to stride out for Flint, following Oakenholt Lane but it does mean considerable road walking ahead, first along the narrow and busy Paper Mill Lane and even more so the dreaded A548. So, to reduce roadwork and continue a more pleasant rural route, when you reach the* end of the driveway from Cheshire Farm turn right and almost immediately discover a footpath going off to the left, which is more of a lane than a path. Go through a gateway into a field. You need to walk due west diagonally across this field and may be helped by a distinguishable cart track, aiming to the left of the power line pole. You have crossed the field now and find another gateway, with a walkers' sign on the left-hand post indicating that next you need to turn left. Keep to the field edge and make for the corner of the field, where you will find a gateway and a sign indicating you must next turn sharp right, which you do, walking along with the hedge to your right. Maintain this course, going through a field gap and continue to the next field corner, which is in fact the junction of three field corners and a gate to your left. Go through the gateway, keep the hedge to your right and a field (*of barley in our case*) on your left. This is a broad pathway, mature oaks to the right and fenced barley to the left. You come to the end of the track into a much larger featureless field.

15 You now face a wood, and that is your destination, although an entry is not easy to find. The woodland is fenced off, so you do need to locate the stile, which is in a corner at the far side of the field. One way to find it is to go straight across the field and then keep right to locate the stile in its obscure corner. Eventually you will come to this, somewhat disabled, stile, with a dodgy step. Cross over and you are in the wood. A pleasant woodland walk follows, although it is probably not walked often and although there is a liberal sprinkling of walkers' signs on posts, the pathway underneath is not always easy to follow. The sound of water leads you a delightful footbridge over a stream with a marker telling you to bear left on the other side. Climb uphill to come out of the wood by way of a new metal stile into a field where you turn half left. Clip the edge of the field, making leftish to a field corner. *It's tempting to think you might be able to make another spirited dash for the estuary by taking a straightforward route via Leadbrook Hall, but there is no public right of way.*

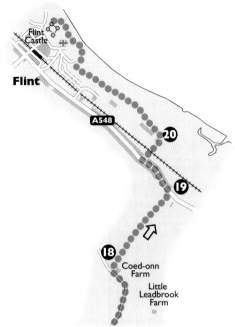

16 So when you reach the field corner, which is the junction of three fields, turn left through the gateway. The arrow of the waymark on the post points to the canopy of a tree ahead, and this is the direction to follow. Go into the field, sloping gently upwards, with the distant estuary now on your right. Go up and straight across towards the tree on the horizon. The field soon slopes gently down to the tree, and beside it a gateway and stile. Go through the gateway and maintain the same direction uphill in the next field. You are aiming for a field corner which you cannot see. Climb gently and make for trees in the woodland coming in from the right. When you reach the brow of the hill you will see the desired field corner, a dead tree pointing towards it, on my last visit. At this corner you will find two stiles, so use the one on the right, taking you in a new direction. Cross over the stile under a new oak, rich with acorns, into woodland. Keep as close to the fence on your left as you can through undergrowth. Use the fence to guide you under trees, including a splendid beech tree, downhill towards a projecting corner. You will eventually gain access into the field on your left, but need to go round the projecting corner to find a yellow-hatted stile. Cross the stile, out of woodland into the field and turn right.

17 Keep the hedge to your right, going ever so slightly uphill, as views open up to the left, to reach a sturdy stile accompanied by a waymark. Once over, you find yourself on a broad track, fence to the left, hedge to the right, and as it swerves suddenly left, go straight on to find a strong new stile, which will help you into the field beyond. Here keep close to the hedge on your right to the next corner, where a yellow-hatted stile leads onto a minor road. Turn right and follow the road. Ignore the road coming in from the left (Llwyn Onn). Under power lines the road narrows and turns sharp left. Go with it, passing the bungalow on your right followed by the ancient farm, Coed-onn. Just after the farm buildings, look out for a waymark on a post, indicating 'Oakenholt ½ mile' and mount old steps to a stone stile into a field.

18 Once in the field, and with farm buildings on your right, progress down towards the estuary, keeping close to the right hand hedge. You see a stile ahead in the field corner, with a walker's sign curiously placed at ground level, though this tells you that you need to keep the hedge on your right in the next field. Do this, to reach the next field corner and

33

a double stile leading into the final field, again keeping the hedge to your right. At the next field corner, with an open gateway to the right cross directly via a stile into what until recently was a field, but is now a building site. *New houses are springing up, and by the time you read this may well be finished.* I followed the temporary pedestrian route, well managed, through the site to reach a pavement and houses now complete. Follow the pavement down, looking out for what is at present a green path leaving the site and make for the road. So, after the new housing you pass old housing on the left and arrive at a stile which brings you onto the snarling main road, where you turn left. You are now on the Wales Coast Path, or Coast Road, I should say, walking into Flint.

19 Keep on the left-hand side pavement, passing the Yacht Inn on the right and a church, on your left, which is itself more like a building site, and may well be something other than a church when you come this way. Look out for a speed camera on the right and at this point cross the road, when you can find a space in the traffic, (*this is really busy, particularly if you approach Flint at rush hour*) towards a bus stop and bus shelter. Just beyond you leave the road, using the fingerpost sign, right, to take you through a gate TO WALK over the railway line (this is the main London to Holyhead line – do look both ways) and proceed safely through the gate on the other side. Make for a gate which leads into a field and beyond that the mudflats and marshlands of the estuary. Keep the field edge on your left and pass through an old hedgerow line to bring you out onto the estuary proper, with a waymark on a post.

20 In wet or misty weather the next move might be difficult to follow. After the waymark, head out, half left, as if making for the river. If visibility is good you will see a low mound, which is a useful marker. You may be on mudflats, but the surface is quite green. Make for the mound and you should see duckboards appearing. Use the duckboards to go past the mound, on your right, and in between two posts. The path takes you next over a footbridge, fenced to each side. The path now decides to go back inshore more, leftish. As you approach a hedgerow you come to another footbridge, and the castle is now in full view ahead, apparently close to a prominent display of floodlights over the rugby pitch. The footpath keeps close to the hedge, through a marshy patch, a waymark with a yellow arrow taking you to a kissing gate. This means you leave the estuary now to follow a path on relatively dry land. You reach a junction of paths and turn right. This distinct grey path winds its way round the edge of the foreshore, dog roses in full bloom. If you have time, there is an information board over to your right, giving a description of bird life on this precious Dee estuary, but you may want to be galloping ahead to the finishing line now. Go through a gateway, narrow at the top and turn left on a broad tarmac path which will take you to the castle, now prominently in view. Past the rugby pitch you come to car park and from here you can successfully scramble over the (dry) moat to wander round the Castle at leisure. The castle is not far from the railway station, if you left your car there, and close to the town itself.

5 FLINT CASTLE to Bailey Hill,
Mold, via Hen Blas Castle (site only)

Flint Castle

Begun in 1277, Flint Castle on the Dee Estuary was one of the first to be built in Wales by Edward I, changing hands between the Welsh and English, later being used by Henry Bolingbroke to force the deposition of Richard II.

Discover a secluded valley on the Wat's Dyke Way as you cross fields and parkland to reach the site of a long-lost castle perched on Bailey Hill in Mold.

Distance: 13 miles
Gradient: Some climbing away from the estuary, but mostly level
Terrain: Early built-up section with roads, giving way to fields, paths and woodland
Rating: Moderate

Once away from the built-up coastal strip, this walk follows a particularly fine stretch of woodland valley and stream, along Wat's Dyke Way, before a rural stretch of field and parkland

1 Leave Flint Castle and enter Castle Walk to follow the path signposted 'Wales Coast Path' seawards, winding round with captivating views of the Estuary, mudflats,

and the surging tide. The path soon takes a more inland route to follow the edge of what was originally Flint Dock, (*see the information panel)* long gone, emerging on the other side to pick up the path again through a gateway onto Flint Foreshore. Keep going towards the estuary and follow the coastal path. You now have the estuary on your right. When the path divides, take the left-hand one, but resist the temptation to join the statue of the man in armour over to the left, although you are looking out for a path which takes you away from the coast. Go through a kissing gate and bear left to reach an aluminium gate and kissing gate beside it, which is the route to take inland.

2 Ignore a path off to the left and continue ahead, signed Bagillt, through a kissing gate to arrive at the railway line protected by a wooden gate. WALK

ACROSS THE RAILWAY LINE, this, the main London-Holyhead line no less, (take care) to the wooden gate on the other side, and then a kissing gate which brings you out onto the industrial estate by the side of the dual carriageway, the A 548. Cross the dual carriageway with care, and on the other side turn right to continue along the pavement for a while. Eventually the route detaches itself from the dual carriageway, mercifully, onto the old road with pavement on both sides. You slip into a service road called Reynolds Road, and at the end of this road turn sharp left into Manor Drive, which comes to an end as it reaches the countryside.

3 Turn right, but not through the green metal gate into the play area. Follow the path between the play area, now on your left and fenced off houses to your right. The path gives a shake and you now have a fence on your left, bringing you to a lane, which you cross, up the other side through a gate into a field which you also cross. Step through an old field boundary and make for a field corner slightly up to your left, where a kissing gate will bring you out onto the edge of a relatively new housing estate. *The next section is difficult to negotiate, as this new housing has been superimposed on old pathways.* So the first thing to find is a three-way walkers' sign on a post, although this proves to be only relatively helpful. You need to follow the central sign which seems to be pointing vaguely up and through houses. To comply with this directive you need to go up the 'road' uphill, keeping Old Orchard to your left and very soon afterwards take an unmarked path off to the left. This 'path' backs onto the back garden of Old Orchard. There is no sign, though one would be useful. As you pass between houses, up towards a field, you will eventually find another heavily disguised and narrow pathway, by taking a sharp right turn up

against the field boundary. You are now on the promised path, poorly signed, between the field on your left and the backs of houses on your right. You come to a more open area, bear round, rightish and a stile and a public footpath sign lead you into a play area. Carry on through this playground with a forbidding high metal fence on the left, until you reach a stile providing safe passage through the said forbidding fence. Avoid the metal kissing gate on the right-hand side of the playground. After the stile, turn sharp left into a field, now walking with a hedge on the left, as if back towards Flint. The built-up section is now behind you.

4 Your straight route takes you through three or four fields with stiles in the field corners. In the final field aim for a prominent tree ahead. Here it looks as if the path is dipping down to cross another field boundary, but instead of doing that, change direction. As you begin the descent of the slope, avoid going into the corner of the field but turn sharp right and go significantly uphill with your current field on the right, and stream and emerging woodland on the left. This is about as close as you get to the site of Hen Blas Castle. You reach a stile, which would do justice to the Grand National, and continue upwards, still with woodland to the left and an expanse of field on the right, keeping to the left-hand edge of the field. There is a prominent small hill emerging ahead, which you keep on your left. When you reach the field corner, you gain access into the next field, turn right and follow the field edge to the far corner where there is a stile. Once in the next field turn sharp left and continue upwards along the field edge which veers round to the right, until you come to the final field corner where there is a gate leading onto a road. Here you turn left, uphill, to experience a stretch of road walking.

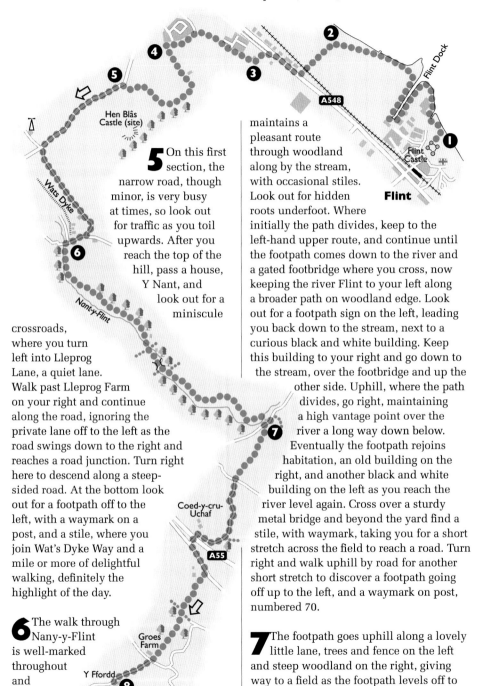

5 On this first section, the narrow road, though minor, is very busy at times, so look out for traffic as you toil upwards. After you reach the top of the hill, pass a house, Y Nant, and look out for a miniscule crossroads, where you turn left into Lleprog Lane, a quiet lane. Walk past Lleprog Farm on your right and continue along the road, ignoring the private lane off to the left as the road swings down to the right and reaches a road junction. Turn right here to descend along a steep-sided road. At the bottom look out for a footpath off to the left, with a waymark on a post, and a stile, where you join Wat's Dyke Way and a mile or more of delightful walking, definitely the highlight of the day.

6 The walk through Nany-y-Flint is well-marked throughout and

maintains a pleasant route through woodland along by the stream, with occasional stiles. Look out for hidden roots underfoot. Where initially the path divides, keep to the left-hand upper route, and continue until the footpath comes down to the river and a gated footbridge where you cross, now keeping the river Flint to your left along a broader path on woodland edge. Look out for a footpath sign on the left, leading you back down to the stream, next to a curious black and white building. Keep this building to your right and go down to the stream, over the footbridge and up the other side. Uphill, where the path divides, go right, maintaining a high vantage point over the river a long way down below. Eventually the footpath rejoins habitation, an old building on the right, and another black and white building on the left as you reach the river level again. Cross over a sturdy metal bridge and beyond the yard find a stile, with waymark, taking you for a short stretch across the field to reach a road. Turn right and walk uphill by road for another short stretch to discover a footpath going off up to the left, and a waymark on post, numbered 70.

7 The footpath goes uphill along a lovely little lane, trees and fence on the left and steep woodland on the right, giving way to a field as the footpath levels off to join a broad farm track. Follow this up to a road junction. Go straight across here, keeping to the track until you reach a four-way road junction. Continue straight ahead and this road will take you via a bridge over the bellowing A55. Once over the bridge you reach a proper main road where you turn left along the pavement to follow a straight stretch of road for a while, looking out for a bridleway, signed, off to the right. This will take you uphill to a road junction and post 69, where we leave Wat's Dyke Way and turn left. After a short distance, only 5 paces, look out for a footpath going off to the right, which uses a very civilized, but hidden, stile, with steps, to bring you into a field. Walk down to the stream and cross via a footbridge, just a plank of wood, and up the other side to another stile which will bring you into a sloping field. You cannot see your exit point as you set off, which is a field corner, left, by the side of a copse and to the left of a small section of projecting field. Here there is a stile taking you into another field inhabited by low, portable, sheds (*empty on our visit*). The route keeps power lines to the left, as you aim for the left hand side of the building ahead, Groes Farm. At the far side of the field pass more sheds, to reach a field gate, or pair of gates and a little brook to cross into another field. Continuing with your planned route go uphill, and at the top find a stone stile, and a public footpath sign. Once over you find you have a three-way road junction. Choose the road straight ahead.

8 Pass a house, Y Ffordd, and leave the road, left, along a track making for Caerfallwch Farm. Keep the farmhouse and then the duck pond on the left and reach a yard and cowshed. Go right, round the cowshed, but keep as close to it as you can and on your left, because your next decision is to make a choice between two fields. Resist the temptation to choose the easy option of a right hand field gate, and instead opt for the harder one, a smaller gate into the lefthand field. The main point is to be in a field where the hedge is on your right. Keep relatively close to the hedge here, and as it turns sharp right follow it to look out for a stile with two platform steps which enables you to reach a road. Turn left on the road to Tyddyn-bâch which soon appears on your left. There is something of a corkscrew movement required now. Use the road to go past Gwern Y Fynnon, a handsome stone building, on the right, and almost immediately pick up a path off to the right which brings you to a superb stone stile. Cross here and turn sharp left, before needing to find a footpath off to the left yet again. After the gate, avoid the paved road and turn left immediately into the field as you pick up Wat's Dyke Way again.

9 Your route now takes you across five fields, with stiles, always keeping to the left-hand field edge where a brook accompanies you, the last stile bringing you out onto a road. Cross the road, to locate a metal stile on the other side guiding you into the field beyond. You now have the brook and field edge on your right before reaching a stile in a fence facing you. You are now in a large odd-shaped field, narrow at first, opening out. Aim for the prominent oak tree ahead where there used to be a field boundary, but is no more. When you reach the tree, turn sharp left (while Wat's Dyke Way goes straight ahead) and make for a stile in the field boundary facing you. Once over the stile turn right along a farm track heading down to Sarn Galedd, with land sloping sharply away to your left. On the horizon you may be able to make out Beeston Castle and the sharp turret of Castle Cement looking like something out of Cape Canaveral. You are now in the farmyard of Sarn Galedd, alive with friendly dogs, and beyond that, through

Caerfallwch

Gwern y Ffynnon

Tyddyn-bâch

9

the right-hand of two gates, go down a sloping field towards a metal stile at the bottom. Cross into a very marshy area. Pick any suitable route to the far side and a broken stile giving way to a drier field. In this field

Sarn Galedd

Quarry Farm

10

Ram Wood

Gwysaney Hall

keep the power lines and hedge to your left as you make for Quarry Farm but turn right virtually at the field edge and turn 90 degrees, making for Gwysaney Hall, hidden in the woods beyond.

I O Keep the fence to your left, but avoid going through the entrance to another field which slopes dramatically downwards. You reach the field corner complete with gate and stile. Cross over into Ram Wood and continue along the track ahead to a five-barred gate with kissing gate to the right. Follow the prominent stone wall on the left and Scots Pine on the right with an open field beyond. You reach another metal gate, and kissing gate to the right, to walk into woodland. On reaching the pool, go left along the cart track which skirts the Hall on the left. Avoid going

11

A541

River Alyn

A5119

Mold

A541

left into the Hall grounds after the pool. You should now be walking through parkland with impressive trees to reach a T-junction, where you take the lefthand road, as if taking you to the main entrance of Gwysaney Hall, whose impressive frontage now appears. You then follow a track, right, downhill, through, or beside, a spanking new five-barred gate across the drive. Descend to a house, on the left. Pass through a gate across the drive, with a waymark on a post and reach a road. Turn right and walk along the road.

I I The town of Mold and particularly St Mary's Church gradually come into view. As the road goes over a bridge across a stream, you will see a complex of buildings to your left, which you make for, now leaving the road. A walkers' sign guides you, vaguely, towards an electricity sub-station, but just when you reach its formidable fence you will see a cunning path off to the right. Cross a stile and turn left. You now have the sub-station on your left and the River Alyn/Afon Alyn on your right. The field you are in is often susceptible to flooding and can be moist and marshy. Keep the river on your right, flowing in your direction, and the long path, if path there is, will bring you to the main road into Mold. The way out of the field, by the way, is not near the river, but on a prominent stepped stile midway along the side of the road. Once on the main road turn right into the town. Walk on the pavement to a roundabout, cross and continue along King Street to the town centre. To reach Bailey Hill, the site of a long-lost Norman castle, turn right at the traffic lights and continue up High Street, past the church on your right, to find the entrance to Bailey Hill facing you.

39

6 MOLD, Bailey Hill, to RUTHIN CASTLE
Stage one: Mold to LOGGERHEADS

Bailey Hill

The original Norman Motte and Bailey, dating from 1140, passed into Welsh and English hands before being burned down by Llywelyn some fifty years later, and is now being developed as an historical and recreational facility with a Gorsedd Stone Circle incorporated.

A gentle ramble to the famous lead mining Leete Path beside the River Alyn among the trees in Loggerheads.

Distance: 4½ miles
Gradient: Gentle climb up from Mold
Terrain: Fields giving way to woodland
Rating: Easy

With a steep climb up Moel Famau late in the day, the walk from Mold to Ruthin may be too long (16+ miles) to accomplish in one day, unless you relish a stern challenge. So the trail is divided into two stages. There is a bus service

from Mold to and from Loggerheads, with a useful (not free) car park at Loggerheads Country Park, and if based in Mold I would suggest driving to Loggerheads and catching the early commuter bus (service no 1 from Ruthin) into Mold to complete the walk to Loggerheads.

If you are based in Ruthin, and want to do the whole section, catch the same early bus from Ruthin to Mold. If you then make a decision to cut short your Mold-

Loggerheads
Country Park

Ruthin walk, you can catch a bus from Loggerheads to Ruthin. Once committed to the Loggerheads to Ruthin section of the walk, though, there are no buses en route beyond Loggerheads.

I Leaving the site of the former castle in Mold on Bailey Hill, turn sharp right at the road junction into Pwll Glas and walk along the pavement. Not far along find a narrow alleyway going off down to the left, indicated by a waymark on a post. This path, bordered by a wall on the left and a fence on the right, takes you down towards Mold Community Hospital, on the right, but misses it, using an entrance drive to emerge onto Elm Drive, by the community centre, where you turn right.

2 Follow Elm Drive round, as it bears left, into the housing estate and continue along the pavement, with houses on both sides. You reach a right-hand bend in Elm Drive where you need to look out for a pathway, left, with privet hedges to both sides. At the end of this pathway confront a high metal gate providing access into countryside.

3 You are in a field now, and need to keep the right-hand hawthorn hedge to your right, continuing until you reach a prominent tree with a field gate, on your right, padlocked on my last visit. Climb over to reach a narrow strip of field on the other side. Turn left. Keep the field edge

to your left, until it curls round, right, and here you will find an overgrown kissing gate beside a field gate taking you into the next field. The land slopes down towards you from the right, but continue with the field edge and brook on your left, *ignoring a prominent field gate*. The field you are in narrows and almost tapers to a point, where there is a stile by the side of the field gate, bringing you out onto a lane. You are now in Lôn Maes Garmon. Note the waymark on a post on the far side of the gate. Turn left along the lane, which goes uphill, hedges to both sides. At the top of the hill you reach Hendy Road, where you turn right. Continue along the tarmac road.

4 After you pass a house, Hen Dy, on the left, look out for a footpath going off, left, while Hendy Road bears off to the right. Follow the footpath sign and a stile to enter a field. You need to cross this field slap bang in the middle of

it, uphill, making for a field edge opposite (*totally lost to my vision as I headed for bright November afternoon sun, low down*). Keep the electricity pole well to your left, go under power lines and eventually, at the far side of the field, you will come to a kissing gate. After the gate you will find yourself in a steeper field. The path clips the lower edge of this field, maintaining height, before it reaches a stile in the field edge opposite. Two signs on the stile suggest the path divides, so don't cross the stile. Follow the right-hand route, uphill now, keeping the hedge to your left until you come to the top field corner and a water trough, left. You are channelled here into a narrow strip of grassland before reaching a kissing gate, with steps up to an even narrower alleyway. Walk between two walls, uphill, being steered clear of the private driveway on your right but straight up through neighbouring property to join the drive and eventually, at the top, a road, where you turn right. This is Ffordd Hafod.

5 Carry on along the road until it starts to dip downhill, where you will find a prominent footpath sign on the left, with a waymark on a post taking you along a broad driveway and into a plantation. Don't go too far along the driveway as the footpath goes off, right, (look for the yellow arrow) before coming to the end of woodland at a stile with a waymark. Cross into a field, Go straight over the field ahead, making for the pointed roof of a building which will eventually turn out to be a sub-station. Cross a low field boundary and another field before reaching a stile. A narrow path, with wall on the left and fence on the right brings you in sight of the said sub-station, where you turn distinctly left and cross a stile into another field. Traverse the field, with the summit of Moel Famau at last in view, keeping the electricity pole to your right before going under the power lines. Make for a clump of trees on the left and a stile on your right. Cross the stile and turn left along the path through scrubland. You now come to a track, or lane. Turn left.

6 Follow this access lane into habitation. A waymark on a post in the ground on your left confirms the route, as the lane veers round between houses to reach a junction. Look out for a path, on your right, to the left side of a property called 'Pathside' (*appropriately*). A waymark on a post in the ground directs you along a narrow path between high hedges. This short-lived path brings you to a stile and access into a large field sloping away from you. Make for the opposite field corner, descending the field on the diagonal. You

should be able to see traffic on the road ahead, which is where you want to be. Descend briskly to a wet hollow and up the other side to a stile in the left-hand corner. Once over the stile, climb up steps onto the road, which you cross to find a footpath into woodland edge. Turn left and follow this path.

7 Continue along under the trees, with the road, pretty heavy with traffic, close by on your left. Here you will find Deborah's Well (*she's been off colour recently*). The path divides at this point, so follow the footpath up to the right into woodland, with warning signs reminding you to keep out of the Quarry. So uphill you go to a stile and briefly leave woodland, as the path continues with two fences to the left and brambles and scrubland edge to the right. This level and muddy path re-enters woodland and goes uphill again to a walkers' sign, where the path veers left, levels out, then undertakes a simple descent in distinctive woodland. You now come to a point where the path divides. Although you want to go to Loggerheads, don't take the path off to the right signed Loggerheads. Instead, continue forwards, signed Cadole on a post in the ground. A broad path in woodland continues its pronounced descent. There are many tracks in this well-walked woodland, so avoid paths off to the right and continue ahead to reach habitation and Cadole. When you emerge you will see a kissing gate off to the left. Turn sharp right here, at 90°, along a clear path, bearing left to reach a walkers' crossroads in a clearing. Turn sharp left again, making for what looks like a fence in woodland but turns out to be a short line of metal poles. Through here and you are back in woodland proper, up a slight rise before plunging down more sharply, to the left, where wooden steps appear to help you, as you begin to hear the rumble of traffic on the main Mold to Ruthin road. Just before you come to the array of gates, and the road beyond, turn sharp right.

8 As you turn you will see a sign for Loggerheads Country Park. So continue along this broad path uphill for a while until you reach a well-signed fingerpost, where you turn sharp left and follow the path taking you down the 100 or so steps.

After the steps you eventually arrive at Loggerheads Country Park. It's definitely worth going over the bridge into the Park Centre to grab a welcome breather and refreshments at the excellent Caffe Florence (*open the year round, typically 10 am to 4pm*) This is a useful spot to break your journey, if you think the complete Mold to Ruthin trek is a step too far in one day.

7 MOLD, Bailey Hill, to RUTHIN CASTLE
Stage two: LOGGERHEADS to RUTHIN

A challenging journey to the stark heights of Moel Famau as you pioneer your way over the rolling Clwydian Hills down to the peaceful Vale of Clwyd.

Distance: 11 miles
Gradient: Steep climb up onto the Clwydian Hills
Terrain: Woodland valley giving way to mountain paths
Overall: Strenuous

9 Once refreshed, cross back over the River Alyn the way you came and turn left to follow the river along the enchanting 2 mile Leete Path, initially signed 'Devil's Gorge' In terms of route you make various choices as you go, but basically keep the river always close by on your left as you wind your level way through woodland. You reach the dog's home, on the left, and pass through a kissing gate. Just beyond, use the track away from the property, making sure you leave it by plunging into woodland straight ahead where tracks cross, once again following the sign to Devil's Gorge. As you continue, tracks go off to left and right, but continue ahead, signed Cilcain until you reach the footbridge high over Devil's Gorge. The Leete Path narrows, squirms a bit and eventually reaches a road, which you join

by turning sharp left downhill, signed Cilcain 1 mile.

10 This road crosses the river via a sturdy bridge and climbs up steeply the other side. Avoid the bridle path off to the left by the river, and mount sharply upwards by road until it turns abruptly right. Here there is a footpath, off to the left, with a waymark on a post, where you leave the road. With a garden fence to the right, and a steep drop down to the river on the left, the footpath contours round to a stile which propels you into a field. Keep the field edge to the left and the open field to your right to another stile in the field corner. In the field beyond descend, still with the field edge on your left to the next stile in the field corner. Another field follows, edge to the left, to another corner and a kissing gate. Follow the path through woodland edge to a stile marked Pentre Cilcain, though you are not going there. Cross over the stile to another one close by and follow the usual pattern of field edge to the left and field to the right. The next stile, also marked Pentre Cilcain takes you into woodland. Here the path divides. Don't go left to Pentre Cilcain, but carry on ahead, to Cilcain itself through new woodland. Upwards now, you reach a large gate and

43

beyond that a road, where you turn right This road will bring you up to the centre of the village, a cross roads and the White Horse Inn. Turn left here at this staggered junction of roads.

11 Follow the road upwards, with the church on the left and useful public toilets on the right to reach a road junction where you turn left. Journeying along the road you may spot an elephant in the garden to your left and certainly gain your welcome glimpse of your target, the truncated memorial, Moel Famau, high on the horizon. Continue along the road, downhill to the bottom, and up the other side to a parting of the ways. Cross the bridle way and choose the stony path ahead, through a gateway onto a track. Almost immediately look out for a footpath sign on your right, which will take you off the track via a stone stile and into a field, signposted Clwydian Way.

12 Continue up the field, with the field edge close on the left, to reach a stile in the corner and beyond that a second field, fence to the left, and its marshy corner harbouring a stile into a lane, where you turn left. Almost immediately turn right, as indicated by the blue arrow and follow the lane. You come to a gate and stile to one side. Continue uphill, fence on the left, and the reservoir beyond begins to surface.

13 Go through a gate, following the blue arrow, entering more open moorland, as the obvious path climbs more steeply upwards, past the tree line, notably horse chestnuts. The path has steps and a rail now, so that gives you an idea of the gradient until you eventually reach the corner of a plantation.

14 From the corner of the plantation the only way is up, at first keeping the trees on your left, then through a gate into open country and the climb to the summit. *Moel Famau is always busy, so expect to find lots of walkers up here. It's always very windy, too, in my experience, but take some time admiring the stupendous view of the Vale of Clwyd and the Clwydian hills stretching to both sides.*

15 *To make the descent, just check your bearings, as there are several ways to go, and in mist, after a good wander round Moel Famau, you may be slightly disorientated. In particular, don't take the way down through trees back to Loggerheads. Instead stride out along the clear, well-trodden path to the car park on the col, the well-worn route which may be busy with other walkers, some of whom will be doing Offa's Dyke long-distance footpath which you have now joined.*

11

10

Cilcain

12

13

of Ruthin. You reach another gate across the track, and beyond that a further gate, with a kissing gate by the side bringing you onto a road, where you turn left.

16 You reach a car park, and need to follow the road, right, towards Ruthin, looking out for an early and well-signed bridle path going off to the right. Don't be tempted to stick to this bridle path, though, because when you reach a gate across your route you will see a stile, to the left of it, shorn of signs. This will lead you down steeply to a valley, on your left. Head for the stream.

14

15

Moel Famau Jubilee Tower

After you have completed the steep walk down to the stream, now close by on your left, continue to cross a track, with a faded waymark on a post. Follow the stream, always on your left, making for woodland ahead. Eventually a new wooden footbridge takes you over the water, and a stile, with 'Welcome' on it. You are now in a field which slopes down steeply from the left with the stream over to your right. Eventually you come to a pond, on your right. Here there is a kissing gate taking you into a wood, with a blue marker sign on a post. The path winds its way through woodland. After you pass the house on the left, the path climbs up to join the drive from the house, so keep right here and join the driveway with the stream now some way down to the right. You reach a gate across the track, with a kissing gate to the right, giving you a view of the Vale of Clwyd and your destination, the town

17 Follow the road round Llanbedr Hall Estate to reach more of a main road. Turn right, and almost immediately right again, downhill along the tarmac. This road, Lon Cae Glas, eventually comes out on the busy main road, the A494 which has also found a way over, snaking down from the pass on the Clwydian Hills. Turn right at this main road and walk along the pavement, downhill. Pass the church on the right and cross the road coming in from the right but stay on the same side of the main road. The Griffin Inn is on the other side of the main road. Continue along the pavement for a short while, looking out for a footpath off to the right.

Loggerheads Country Park

9

18 At this point go through a gate inside a gate into the field and make first for the lone tree in the middle. From here continue towards a far field corner, leftish. Cross a stile and make for a gate at the far side of the field. Once through this new kissing gate you come to a lane, to be crossed, and continue down the track ahead towards the farm, Wern. Before you reach the farm though, and just as the

45

track veers sharply to the right, look out for a field gate in the hedge to your left, avoiding the temptation to continue into the field directly ahead. Turn left, through the gate into a field and immediately turn sharp right to follow the field edge, keeping it on your right. Ignore the field gate on the right and continue down to discover a stile in the hedge to your right. Cross here and over a wooden footbridge into the field and turn sharp left down to the field corner, where you will find a stile waiting and a footbridge over the stream. Another stile with a waymark takes you into a field. Keep its edge close to the left. Walk under power lines, cross a ditch, climb a stile, pass under power lines again and you are in the next field. Go straight across here, making for the redbrick buildings of Ruthin School. Once across the field you'll find a gate and stile bringing you onto a metalled road which you cross. Negotiate the stile on the other side of the road, and walk across the next field, approaching the school. The way out of this field is to the right of

the redbrick building, with its diamond decoration, where you will find a stile. The footpath now makes its way between school buildings on the left and mobile classrooms on the right, then through a little gate before the path ends at a road where you turn right. Follow the road, Bryn Goodman, as it bears left, an unadopted road taking you down to Ruthin itself and Greenfield Road.

19 To reach the castle, first of all make for the roundabout ahead, which you need to negotiate with care, left, to cross Station Road and head uphill, Market Street, to the centre of town, the Square. Of all the roads available choose Castle Street, over to the left, and progress to the splendid fortified entrance to Ruthin Castle, now Ruthin Castle Hotel. Check in at reception to let them know you want to look at the ruins and then stroll about to see enchanting remains of a medieval castle.

8 RUTHIN CASTLE to DENBIGH CASTLE

Enjoy the pastoral landscape in the Vale of Clwyd, as you walk along the renowned Lady Baghot's Drive beside the river Clywedog, on your way to the ancient fortress of Denbigh Castle

Distance: 12½ miles
Gradient: Level at first, becoming undulating
Terrain: Fields, paths, minor roads and
          woodland edge
Grade: Moderate

If based in Denbigh for this walk, there is a useful bus service from here to Ruthin which I would recommend doing first thing in the morning. I say this because we

pioneered this route mid-winter, and it is the first walk I've completed by torchlight! I wouldn't recommend approaching Denbigh Castle in the gloaming. Middle sections of this route, I suspect, are not well-walked, so orienteering may well be an issue. Choose one of two routes from Ruthin Castle

1A *If you have been visiting the castle it is possible to make your way down from the Hotel grounds to the river via the Stone Circle, which is visible from the hotel entrance complex. This is not a public right of way, but has the blessing of the proprietors. Go through the kissing gate into the Stone Circle area and descend,*

Ruthin Castle

This 13th century Welsh-built castle, also known as 'the red castle in the great marsh' (Castell Coch yn yr Gwernfor), occupied the site of a Roman fort and was ceded to Edward I in 1277, its ruins now in the grounds of a hotel.

leftish, to a field corner where there is a stone bridge over the river. Cross over onto a public footpath and turn right, following this path with the river on your left and the fence on your right, through a kissing gate and enter a children's play area. Do not cross the river, but continue past the skateboard area and enter a car park, using the pavement to reach the main road, where your turn right. Cross the road and after a short distance pick up a footpath, left, leading over a bridge. Go to **2**.

I B *It is also possible to take a shorter route from the main castle entrance.* Travel along Castle Street as if back into town, but choose a public footpath close by, off left. *This was closed on our visit, owing to a fallen tree, but I guess the path will now be open.* Follow this path, called Cunning Green, to the road at the bottom and turn right. Continue along the road, Mill Street, to the main road, Heol Clwyd, and turn left, cross the road to pick up the footpath, now on your right, over a foot bridge.

2 This will bring you out onto a car park. Walk through here on a walkway, the river now on your right. At the end of this stretch you reach the main road where you turn right, keeping to the pavement until you cross the river, when you need to go over the busy main road, A494, to the waymark by the kissing gate, giving access into a field. *You have now completed the tour of Ruthin and head for open country.*

3 Once in the field, almost immediately bear left over a substantial bridge to take you onto the lefthand side of the River Clwyd as it flows towards the sea. The footpath divides here, so turn right as soon as you have crossed the bridge, and accompany the river which is now on your right. After 200 yards or so of riverside field the path divides again, though not obviously. Take the left-hand option. A good direction finder is a tree in the field ahead and beyond that a short feeder slip road, like a ramp, coming into the field from a road ahead.

4 You reach the slip road which is guarded by a padlocked gate, *presenting quite a stern climbing challenge.* Once over the gate, proceed up the driveway to a main road, the A525, cross it and go down the other slip road on the

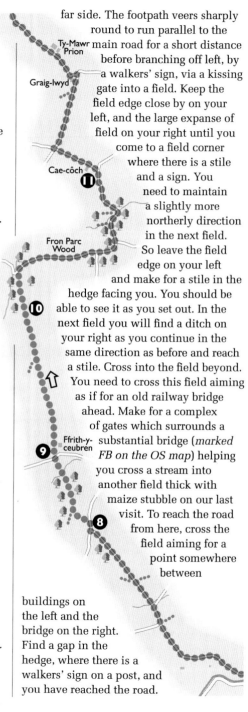

far side. The footpath veers sharply round to run parallel to the main road for a short distance before branching off left, by a walkers' sign, via a kissing gate into a field. Keep the field edge close by on your left, and the large expanse of field on your right until you come to a field corner where there is a stile and a sign. You need to maintain a slightly more northerly direction in the next field. So leave the field edge on your left and make for a stile in the hedge facing you. You should be able to see it as you set out. In the next field you will find a ditch on your right as you continue in the same direction as before and reach a stile. Cross into the field beyond. You need to cross this field aiming as if for an old railway bridge ahead. Make for a complex of gates which surrounds a substantial bridge (*marked FB on the OS map*) helping you cross a stream into another field thick with maize stubble on our last visit. To reach the road from here, cross the field aiming for a point somewhere between buildings on the left and the bridge on the right. Find a gap in the hedge, where there is a walkers' sign on a post, and you have reached the road.

5 Cross the road to a stile. Enter a field and proceed, keeping the field edge to your left, to reach a stile in the corner and a walkers' sign, where you cross into the field beyond. You now have a field edge on your right bringing you to a stile. Clip the next field along a fairly well-trodden path, making for the new housing and a visible, if ramshackle stile into habitation. You are now in Rhewl. Go down Maes Derw to reach Bro Clywedog at a T-junction, where you turn left making for the main road, the A525 again. At the main road turn right, following the pavement past the Drovers' Arms and bus stop, cross the road to find a walkers' sign on a post guiding you away from the main road. You go over the river, Afon Clywedog, and follow the drive round to the left, marked by a walkers' sign on a post. You are now on the Clwydian Way, the river flowing swiftly, left, field and woodland on the right.

6 A very pleasant 2-mile walk follows through woodland, along what is known locally as Lady Bagot's Drive, with the river always on your left. So keep to the lower and riverside path where there is a choice, although you will find that you are climbing almost imperceptibly as you go. After this delightful riverside walk you come to a gate and a road beyond.

7 Turn left here and continue, downhill at first, along the road until you come to a junction on a hill close to houses. Turn right at this point and follow the road, houses to the right and the river

a distant memory over to the left. The road climbs, quite sharply at times, and this becomes your route now for more than a mile. It's a quiet road most of the time, but narrow, so keep your ears tuned for the surprise of white van man. Continue uphill, ignoring waymarked paths and roads off. You will eventually discover a road coming in from the left (*it actually comes in twice*) and soon after the second road junction take a waymarked footpath, signed, off to the left.

8 So leave the road now, go down and cross the rather high stile to reach a sloping field. *In this next section you need to keep your wits about you, as the route is ambiguous at times. To put it mildly.* After leaving the road, keep the field edge to your right to find a field gate at the bottom, also on your right. Go through, and once in the next field, keep the hedge to your left and make for a stile visible in the hedgerow. Once over the

stile continue ahead to reach an old uprooted hedge. Turn right here and follow the line of stumps to woodland. You reach the field corner and cross into the wood via a stile. The way through the wood may seem to be difficult, marshy and vague. We followed some garish yellow ribbons tied to trees, (*are they still there?*) giving way to a red ribbon (*did the trailblazer run out of yellow ribbons, I wonder?*)

49

If still there, these markers will help you to get through the wood to a waymark and a stile. *Real Hansel and Gretel stuff.* You are now in a field which has been recently divided into two fields and this presented us with a navigational problem. You really need to reach a stile, on the far side of the field and somewhat uphill. However this would seem to involve clambering over the new fence, left, which runs across the field, dividing it in two, the one you are in being a rectangular paddock. A way round this is to carry straight on through this paddock to a gate onto a road where you can turn left uphill to reach the target stile. However the official footpath definitely seems to go over the fence, though no stile is discernible. There is a clear fingerpost once you reach the target stile, confirming you are on the Mynydd Hieraethog Trail. On the other side of the road, here, find the next stile to continue your journey, and you are back in the fields.

9 Walk across the next field keeping another new fence and the property Ffrith-y-ceubren on your right to a field corner and a stile, with a useful dog-flap. If you have a dog with you. In the subsequent field keep the hedge to your left, glancing across to view the superb Clwydian hills on the far side of the Vale. In the next field corner you face two gates. Take the left-hand gate into the upper field and follow the field edge which is now on your right. You reach a stile by a gate in the field corner, and once in the next field make for another stile in the far corner. Once over this, you are in a lane. Cross the lane to face two gates. Take the right-hand gate and you are now in a field where you can continue with the field edge on your left. Once through the gate you are in a massive field. Keep close to the hedge to your left which becomes a fence, while looking for a way out. Just past the windswept tree on the left followed by gorse, there is a gate

and a waymark on a post taking you out of one field into another. Once through the gate turn sharp right keeping the gorse hedge on your right as the field slopes steeply away to your left. You come to a fence in a field corner and a stile, helping you into the field beyond. This is an odd-shaped field, sloping away to the left and ahead, with fencing to the right. Leave the field edge now and bisect the field, aiming for woodland ahead and down below. You are on the top of a hill. Descend, and as your way down becomes clearer you will see fir trees appearing in the medium distance. Downhill you continue in a wide expanse of field, with two more prominent trees to the right. You are aiming for the evergreen firs and a way into the wood. As you approach this barrier of woodland you should be able to see a stile midway. Sure enough here it is, and now you can climb over into woodland.

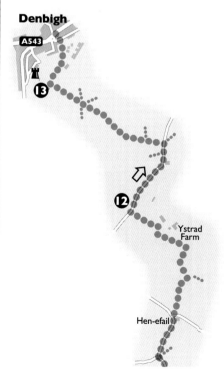

50

10 As you enter the wood, look out for a low level electric fence and a high-level plastic bird of prey. Keep these two deterrents to your left and walk for a short distance to reach a forest ride, where you turn right. Follow this track for a while until it bends sharply downhill to the left. As you descend you will reach a turning circle for vehicles and here a footpath plunges down ahead back into woodland proper. Once through this stretch of woodland you reach a road where you turn sharp right. Follow the road on its up and down way until woodland appears to come to an end on your left. Here you will find a waymark and a footpath to your left, guarded by an old-fashioned gate. You are now back in woodland, Fron Parc Wood, and descend steadily to reach a forest ride. You need to go sharply off to your right here, avoiding the tempting broad pathways to pick up an uphill track through woodland. *Sharp right, remember.* The path then bears left, uphill, with a stream on the right. You come out of the wood at a stile, with waymark, and cross the stream on a low level footbridge of sorts, uphill in the field, with the field edge to your right. The footpath now becomes a lane, or overgrown gulley, *where we found an injured owl even more disorientated than we were,* before reaching a stile at the top. Through a gate you now enter more of a lane, and continue up to the road where you turn left. *That marks the end of a somewhat complicated section. Some road work to come.*

11 Follow the tarmac to a crossroads where you turn right to Graig-lwyd and turn left (with a signpost to Denbigh). Follow the road, turning right at a junction to reach Hen-efail. Here you will find yourself at a T-junction, and you need to pick up the footpath on the other side of the road. The waymark is not easy to see. *Do not be tempted to go down the obvious driveway ahead of you, as we did, because*

this will prove to be a false trail. Instead, find the footpath in the hedge to the right of the drive, and this will take you directly into a field. Keep the hedge to your left and you will reach holiday cottages. Clip the field, and find, close to the cottages, a stile into the next field. Keep the hedge to your left all the way round this field until you reach a stile in the corner. Cross over and turn sharp left, following two sides of this field to the far corner. Here there is a gate, on your left, and you change direction. In the next field keep the hedge closely on your right until you come to a field corner, a waymark, a stile and gate. Once through you are on a track where you turn right, making for Ystrad Farm. The lane turns into concrete and you keep the pond and Farm on your right to pick up a driveway to a proper road where you turn right.

12 This road brings you down and over the river. Look out for a footpath on the left, not the first footpath signed, but the second. Leave the road now and rejoin the Clwydian Way by means of a stone and metal stile onto a footpath comfortingly marked 'To Denbigh Castle'. In the field, keep the fenced edge to your left to make your way upwards to the field corner and a kissing gate. In the next field again keep the hedge and field edge to your left, the castle in full view. You reach a field corner, a gate and a kissing gate. *If you had been with us on our journey into nightfall, you would have found two well-informed guides in luminous hi-viz jackets at this point, helping us pioneer a route through gathering darkness. If you are planning this day's walk in the depths of winter, make sure you have enough daylight! We ran out.* So clip the field you are in along a worn diagonal path to reach an opening in the hedge at the other side of the field. Go through a conspicuous kissing gate, here, into another field. Again you clip the field, leftish on the diagonal, and you should be able to see the next kissing gate you are making for. Pass a field gate on your left. Aim for the next gate in the field corner, with a prominent white-fronted building in the middle distance, a useful pointer. You reach the field gate and a stile by the side taking you into another field. Keep the field edge to the left, passing under power lines. You will reach another field corner, where there is a gate and another stile to the left of the gate. Continue with the field edge to your left to reach a field corner, and steps up to a kissing gate. You are now in your last field, which you need to cross on the diagonal, upwards, along a well-worn path,

hopefully still well-worn. You are aiming for the top right-hand corner of this field. In this field corner find another kissing gate into more of an overgrown patch, with a frighteningly high fence on your right. Follow a path close to said frightening fence to reach woodland. You are now in castle territory and need to turn right.

13 From here follow the path which is at times close to the castle walls on your left, uneven at first but yielding to tarmac, as a well defined track takes you upwards to the town and castle of Denbigh.

9 DENBIGH CASTLE to BODELWYDDAN CASTLE en route for RHUDDLAN CASTLE

Follow old tracks through fields and woodland to find your first fantasy castle at Bodelwyddan, before crossing the River Clwyd to the medieval stronghold at Rhuddlan

Distance: 13 miles
Gradient: Mostly on the level
Terrain: Fields and lanes
Level: Moderate

I Leave Denbigh Castle on Castle Hill, to drop down, by way of a steep and stepped tarmac path, shortly to pick up a similar path off to the right, skirting the castle walls. The tarmac gives way to a more uneven surface as you round the castle wall. You reach the point where you perhaps came in from Ruthin Castle on a previous walk and rejoin the Clwydian Way. Press on ahead, slightly uphill, leaving the castle on the right, until you

reach a road. Turn right on this road, the B4501 and almost immediately turn left. Signs say 'Town Centre', though you're not going there. You are, in fact, on a circular walk avoiding the town centre. Walk along the pavement between houses of Llewellyn Estate, keeping to the side of the road as it begins to descend. Take the first road off left, Bron Castell, and follow it round, looking for a footpath going off right, between two houses, No 24 and No 25. This path takes you round behind the houses to a kissing gate, which leads into open territory and a field. Keep the field edge to your left to reach a field corner. Cross the next field on the diagonal, making as if for a point to the left of the striking black and white building, which is in fact Galch Hill on the map. In the field corner cross over a wooden and stone stile and enter a lane. Here you turn right.

Denbigh Castle

Built on the site of a former Welsh castle, Denbigh is a further example of the imperialism of Edward I, its buildings at the top of the town dominated by an impressive triple-towered gatehouse.

2 You seem to be heading for Galch Hill, but look out for a footpath on the right and go through a kissing gate to enter a field. Follow the field edge round, left, to the field corner. Discover a footpath off to the right, which winds its way between hedges. At the end of this footpath you come to a kissing gate and a lane. At the finger post turn left to follow a broad footpath through woodland edge. After you leave Mount Wood the path will take you to a metal kissing gate and beyond that a main road, where you turn right. You will see now that you have been negotiating a walkers' by-pass of Denbigh. You have a good view of Denbigh Castle up on the hill to your right. Walk along the main road for a short distance before turning off on the metalled track to Lodge Farm.

3 As you approach the impressive façade of Lodge Farm, don't miss a footpath into the field to your left, involving a scramble up into the hedgerow to find a stile. Turn right in the field, keeping the field edge and farm to the right, to reach the field corner and another stile. Once over, make for a gate and adjacent stile, and beyond them a hedge-lined lane, slightly uphill. At the end of the lane cross the stile and turn sharp right. Another lane takes you to the main road, but just before you get there, turn left by the sign into a field. You are making for a gate at the far side of the next field, just in front of a wood. Go through a kissing gate, (the field has been divided), keeping in the same direction to discover a stile at the edge of the wood. You are now in woodland, with a golf course unexpectedly appearing over to your right. Follow the path through woodland edge. You come to a gate. Bear left, still along woodland edge. The next feature is more of a gap in the wall, rather than a gate. You now cross a field, making for a fine single holly tree, more conspicuous than the waymark on a post beside it. Foxhall is over to your right, so make for a stile, right-ish, closer to the house. This stile has no step, but the gate by the side takes you into the working field beyond. It is not easy to see the exit point now, so make for the stone wall ahead, which encircles the old house, Foxhall Newydd, keeping the wall to your left, until you see a stile in the corner over to the right, where stone walls come together. In the next field keep the stone wall to your left, until it becomes a fence, with a waymark on a post in the ground. The village ahead comes into view. Go through a patch of woodland, leaving via a stone stile into what you might call a pitted field. The footpath now follows the right-hand edge of the field as it tapers to a corner, where a stile brings you onto a lane. You have reached Henllan.

4 Follow the lane down into the centre of the village and a convenient shop if

you are short of supplies. At the junction turn sharp right uphill into Church Street, which will take you to the tower, standing on its own, away from the church. Turn left here and follow the main road down, signed Lannefydd. You reach the river at the bottom and the

Glascoed

Sinan

Cefn Meiriadog

Ysgubor Newydd

site of the old mill. There is a tantalising prospect of walking along Afon Meirchion, but sadly there is no public access at this point, so you need to continue uphill on the road. The road divides. Take the one marked to Bont Newydd. Again there is a missing link to a walk through the woods, so continue along this road, ignoring the drive to Coed on the right. We leave the Clwydian Way now. When you reach a point where the road dips slightly down to a stream, look out for a gate to the right. There is a public footpath here, not signed, (though there is a sign at the end, as you will discover) and the footpath is clearly marked on the map, if not on the ground. Therefore turn off the road here, right, and go through the gate.

6 Bont-newydd

Pentre-du Canol

5

5 In the field, keep the fence close by on the right to reach a field corner and what appear to be sheep pens. Go through a field gate here and beyond the pens another gate, taking you down through undergrowth (quite a lot of 'growth' and a certain amount of 'under') to a gully and a stream. Scramble down to the stream, turn right and scramble up again the other side and contrive a passage through a gate. Stiles would definitely be useful on this stretch. As you enter the next field on the rise, keep the field edge to your left. You are making for farm buildings now, with a glimpse of a solitary wind vane over to the left. In the field corner go through a gate and bear right. As you approach the buildings you pass through a gate and make your way up to the old cottage, Pentre-du-canol. The right of way here passes between the cottage on the right and a garage on the left to reach a lane, where, lo and behold you will find a footpath sign on a post pointing the way you have come. You were right after all. No use fretting, though, so turn left and press on along this access lane as it makes its way to a main, if minor, road. Good views on this section of the Clwydian hills on the far side of the Vale of Clwyd. The access lane ends at a T-junction, where you turn right and follow the road to Bont-Newydd, to cross the Pilgrim's Way, and the river, before going up the other side. This is Bont-Newydd.

6 The road bears left, uphill and at a junction veers left again, still on a road before a footpath, right, lets you dive off into woodland. This footpath proceeds parallel to the road for a while but then climbs more steeply through woodland. At the top of the hill the path levels out and reaches a new well-made stile taking you onto a road, where you turn left. A fairly long spell of road walking follows, though the first section, to Glascoed, is along relatively minor roads. When you reach a T-junction turn left and follow the yellow road to Glascoed. The road ends as it faces the imposing, if rather pretentious lodge gate of Bodelwyddan Castle. Unfortunately there is no right of way here to the castle, which is a pity as it necessitates road walking on a much busier and at times narrow and therefore dangerous main road.

7 Turn left at the lodge but not along the B5381. Instead follow the road from the lodge to a junction, turn right and continue down along this perilous main road. There is barely enough room for two-way traffic, let alone walkers, so be prepared to take refuge in the side of the road, as traffic hurtles past. You will be relieved to find the entrance to Bodelwyddan Castle on a dangerous bend, off to the right, and equally relieved to be off the main road and walking through the grounds.

55

BODELWYDDAN CASTLE to RHUDDLAN CASTLE

Bodelwyddan Castle

You may want to include a visit to the 19th century 'castle', here, or take advantage of its toilets and café. There is an entrance charge to the castle.

8 When continuing the walk, follow the entrance road downhill towards the noise of the A55. You can see the Marble Church now, which is your next target. Once you reach the main public entrance to Bodelwyddan castle your next task is

to negotiate a way over the A55. Yes, the A55 is back again. Do this by crossing the slip road and then using the roadway over the trunk road, bearing right to a scary roundabout on the other side to negotiate your walk to the Marble Church, along Rhuddlan Road. *Marble refers to the colour of St Margaret's Church, by the way, not to the building material.* Cross over to the pavement on the left hand side and make for the Church, *which is well worth a visit, if you have time, particularly to see the Commonwealth War Graves of mostly Canadian soldiers who died in the First World War. Thereby hangs a tale. As you will see from the information panel.*

9 Pass the church to a roundabout and a road beyond, looking out for a footpath starting in a hedge to your left, with a waymark on a post. Once over the stile, you need to bear much more to the left than you might imagine to cross the field. Make for an electricity pole in the hedge to the left, which does not appear on the map, rather than going straight across. Close to the electricity pole you will see a post in the fence, with a yellow sleeve on it, and here there is a stile taking you into the field beyond. Make for a field corner, crossing the field on the diagonal to another post with a yellow sleeve. Cross this stile and now keep the next field edge close on the right-hand side. Another stile beckons, with a similar yellow-sleeved marker post enabling you to walk in the next field, now with the field edge to your left. The hedge turns into a fence and you reach another stile, left. Once on top of the stile you will see a

waymark pointing you sharp left, towards the road, which you can reach by following the field edge round to a stile. Once over, and on the main road, turn right. Cross the road, with care – *this is the main entrance to the Hospital* – and follow the pavement and cycleway towards Rhuddlan. Where the cycleway crosses over to the other side it's a good idea to do the same and continue walking along by the side of the road, past Sarn Farm on the right, looking out for a bus stop on the other side of the road,

before you reach power lines. You should be able to see a footpath sign on the hedge on the other side of the road.

10 Cross over the road, looking out again for speeding traffic, to reach the footpath sign and a stile here, helping you into a field. *Stiles and footbridges on the following section of the walk, which I did in late summer, may well be overgrown. I suspect that these paths are not walked often.* Once in the field, make for an exit point in the hedge opposite, keeping Bryn-carrog Farm buildings to your left. You will discover another stile in the hedgerow taking you into the field beyond. Now keep the hedge close by on your left. This field tapers to a corner where there is a gate onto a road facing, almost opposite, two other field gates. Choose the lefthand one, which has a wonky stile to one side. This provides access into a square field. Keep the hedge close by on the right to a field corner and a gate. There is a stile to

57

the right of the gate. *The next section is slightly difficult to negotiate, being low-lying and very wet.* Once over the stile, and eating available blackberries, aim for a footbridge, left-ish, which is not all that easy to identify until you reach it. At first it looks like a set of railings. This takes you over a stream. Bear left and you should see another stile, to your left. It appears to have an electricity pole behind it, which is a good marker. This stile turns out to be the approach to another footbridge. Footbridges are plentiful on this section, which is awash with streams. Cross the footbridge, *more blackberries to eat, plus rabbits, OK to eat if you can catch one.* There is a very good view of your objective, Rhuddlan Castle, ahead. Once in the next field aim for trees ahead, and power lines. The stile, and footbridge you are after, are obscured, but situated in the hedgerow some 20 yards to the right of the trees you can see. Here you can cross the stile and footbridge into the next field. Turn sharp right here and follow the line of hedge on your right to a field corner, and an overgrown stile and footbridge into the final field. You can now see the main road, which you need to reach, after by-passing some discarded picnic tables. Aim for Rhuddlan Castle, flags flying, pass under power lines, cross the field, and make for the road. There is a gateway ahead, and to the right, an obscured stile.

I I When you reach the stile, go over and up steps to reach a thundering dual carriageway. *It is a dual carriageway, so you can cross it in two goes, but if you are reaching this point at the end of the day this may well be full of rush hour traffic.* Once safely over the road a stile will take you into the haven of a Nature Reserve. A metalled walkers' way takes you now between pools and sculptures, bearing right over the old railway line bridge to reach the main road going into Rhuddlan. Turn right here to the town. Just by the traffic lights, from the left-hand pavement, there is a special walkers' footbridge over the River Clwyd. Once over the river, go back to the road up into town and turn right into Castle Street, which will, unsurprisingly, bring you to the Edward 1st Castle *closed during the winter, but still a good view against the setting sun.* There are hostelries and cafés round about, and more places of refreshment in the town itself.

10 RHUDDLAN CASTLE to GWRYCH CASTLE

Enjoy a brisk stroll along the promenade between Rhyl and Abergele to the fantasy castle of Gwrych

Distance: 8 miles
Gradient: Flat
Terrain: Mostly on the promenade
Rating: Easy

The distance between Rhuddlan and Conwy castles (27 miles) is too far to be walked in a single day, though there is a fantasy castle en route, Gwrych Castle, near Abergele. Although, at present, it is possible to approach and view the façade of Gwrych along a private road, there is no public access, nor public right of way, and if a planned hotel project takes off, I guess the road to Gwrych will become closed to everyone except guests. This means that for the purposes of the trail, the best I can recommend is to view the gothic façade

Rhuddlan Castle

Located on an ancient pre-Norman site, the present prominent castle on the edge of the river Clwyd was designed and built by master builder James of St George for Edward I between 1277 and 1282

from the Wales Coast Path, and stop over, or break your journey from Rhuddlan in Abergele. You can go up and view the castle, although this is not a public right of way.

If starting from Abergele, leave your car in the town centre and catch the No 13 bus to Rhuddlan to start your walk there.

From Rhuddlan Castle, retrace your steps down Castle Street and turn left onto the main road. Before reaching the bridge over the river, turn right and follow the tarmac roadway with the river Clwyd flowing urgently on your left. Once you pass the church, on your right, you will come to a junction, and here you need to bear left, (marked Rhyl) and follow the roadway closer to the river and soon under the road bridge. This raised tarmac path, also a cycle way, passes through several gates, as you gain extensive views of the river and its range of geese, swans, shelduck, cormorants and waders. *At the next gate an information board warns you about the effects of flooding in this area.* Once under power lines follow the route and the river seawards. On our last visit the tide turned and the sea starting to swell back inland at this point. Quite fascinating.

2 The tarmac track soon swings away from the river, passes through a gate, then shakes itself back into its original direction. When you reach the chalets, the footpath divides and you need to take the left-hand path, through a gate, following a right-hand fence with chalets beyond. You reach a new pathway development, and signboard (No 84) Take the right-hand route and proceed seawards, as before, to reach habitation. The pathway now becomes a road, with houses to right and left and you can see a footbridge over the railway line, which you need. Cross

with sands and sea to your right as you cross the river Clwyd. To do this you need to turn right over a new bridge system close to a ship's mast replica. This is National Cycle route 5. Turn left, following signs to Kinmel Bay and discover a handy seaside café, The Hub.

Kinmel Bay
A548

North Wales Path

A548

Abergele **4**
A548

Pentre Mawr Park
A55

A547

Gwrych Castle

3 After your coffee break, you will need to follow the footpath towards the sea, with boats to your left, *perhaps including GOLDILOCKS RHYL,* and at the end of this stretch you meet the sea in full force (it can be very windy here) and a signpost allowing you to turn left to Kinmel Bay. There follows a long three-mile tarmac walk and cycleway by the seaside from Rhyl to Abergele, typically with holiday chalets to your left and the sea pounding away on your right. This is the Wales Coast Path. You should begin to see the Gwrych Castle façade on the hillside as you walk towards Abergele. You reach Abergele railway station, on your left, and just beyond a handy promenade with shelters, shops and cafes. *If you stop to eat sandwiches here, beware of Lesser Black-backed gulls, (well, any gulls really) who line up to pounce on unwary feeders. They're not above taking the food out of your very hands. You need to leave the Wales Coast Path here. So....*

over the bridge and on the other side find yourself in another side road, Westbourne Road, making for a main road. Cross this, Wellington Avenue, (*use the pedestrian lights to your left – it can be busy*) and proceed in the same direction as before, making for the promenade, with new retail development in strident blue and white on your left. Cross another main road, West Parade, to reach the promenade. Turn left,

If developments continue as planned, Gwrych Castle will have now become a hotel, and you may want to go there as a guest of the hotel and see the castle remains at the same time. To do this, follow these guidelines.

* When you reach the T-junction on Market Street, turn right and follow the main road, Llandulas Road, to the entrance to Gwrych Castle, which is a prominent (though fake) Norman keep on the corner of the road ahead. Go through the keep entrance and continue along the road to the 'Hotel' and castle. *Please note this is a private gated road and not a public right of way.* A golf course straddles the road, too, to add to the confusion. This existing road continues past the castle (and hotel) into woodland beyond, but none of this is open to the public, which is a pity.

4 Leave the prom and follow the main road, left, over the railway line and then over the A55, using the pavement to enter Abergele. As a change from walking along the road, once over the second bridge you can take the quieter footpath by the side of the rugby pitch in Pentre Mawr park on your left. You will eventually find yourself walking into the residential area of Abergele and a T-junction.* Turn right here, Market Street, for the castle, or left for town centre facilities and your waiting car.

11 GWRYCH CASTLE, ABERGELE, to CONWY CASTLE

Over limestone uplands you follow the North Wales Path to Telford's magnificent suspension bridge and the inspiring towers of Conwy Castle.

Distance: 15 miles
Gradient: Two or three steep climbs
Terrain: Footpaths, fields, limestone and seaside upland, tarmac road finally
Level: Moderate

If you are using just the one car, park in

Abergele and after the walk catch two of the frequent buses back from Conwy to Abergele via Llandudno.

5 Leaving the (*fake Norman*) entrance to Gwrych Castle on your right, walk up Tan-y-Gopa Road as it branches off, right, by the woodland reserve. Keep the castle walls also to your right, passing another impressive (*and also fake*) entrance, on your right, as you forge your way uphill. Observe, but by-pass, a footpath sign to the

61

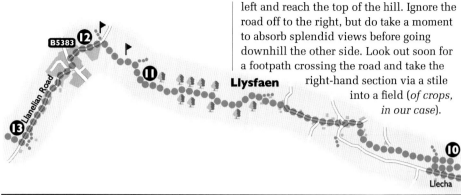

left and reach the top of the hill. Ignore the road off to the right, but do take a moment to absorb splendid views before going downhill the other side. Look out soon for a footpath crossing the road and take the right-hand section via a stile into a field (*of crops, in our case*).

Gwrych Castle

Another fantasy castle, Gwrych was built between 1819 and 1825 and being continually reinvented, hoping now to transmogrify into a hotel and spa.

Pick your way across to a stile in the hedge directly opposite. A white house ahead is a good marker on this section. In the next field, make for an electricity pole at a jutting field corner, and once there keep the hedge on your right to reach a stile in the furthest corner. Over the stile you go, keeping the hedge on your right to a gate and stile into a small field close to the

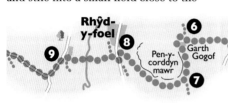

house, and head for the next gate. You have reached Garth Gogof.

6 *The next section of the walk, from Garth Gogof to Rhyd-y-foel is particularly splendid, with panoramic views from the top, and blushing orchids underfoot. But significantly difficult to negotiate. In fact we had to do it twice to get it right (!) Perhaps with these notes you'll have a more trouble-free experience.* The first hazard is to get round Garth Gogof itself which you do by walking away from it at first. Follow the waymark on a post, before plunging off, left, up into undergrowth as you find a way of skirting the house which will now be over to your left. Beyond the outhouse is another gate and stile. Continue downhill, fence to the left and scrubland over to the right. Up above, on the right, is the Pen-y-corddyn mawr massif, with a fort somewhere in there, out of view.

7 You come to a junction, close to a looming rocky bluff up to the right. The path divides here, and it is possible to take the left-hand, longer and lower route, but more rewarding is the right-hand choice. You are going upwards, but not on the perpendicular, circling the rocky hill, as it

were. Coming to a gate, with a stile to the left, proceed upwards, through the gorse, vivid and plentiful on our visit, in April, to reach a more open, closely-cropped surface. It's tempting now to follow this open grassy space to the top, and that's fine, as you look ahead at the great view. *However the way down is much more dodgy, and I suggest two golden rules to help you reach the road at Rhyd-y-foel. The first is not to descend too early; the second is to keep closer to the scree on your right than you would imagine.* So, when you reach the top, turn right to face the mountain. You should see a prominent ash tree between you and the mountain. As you look at the tree you will see, behind it, a fence going up the mountain, another useful visual cue. Make for the ash tree, even if you think you are going in the wrong direction. When you get to the ash tree turn left, keeping the tree and a neighbouring hawthorn on your right and follow, at first, the contours of the hill. There are paths here, through gorse, mostly made by animals. As you walk on you will come to another open space, with the scree tumbling down from the mountain over to your right. There should now appear a cunning little path, rightwards, again making for the scree, taking you away from the open grassy space. You should come to a big boulder, if all goes well. Pass this rock on your right and the path then opens out and becomes much more distinct. Ahead, in the distance, a white fronted house with two chimneys appears, another useful marker. Keep going, downhill now. Hawthorn bushes need to be kept on your right, as you stay close to the scree. Another useful target to make for is a wind-swept rowan tree. As the path

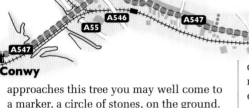

Llandudno Junction

A546

A55

A547

A547

Conwy

A547

A470

approaches this tree you may well come to a marker, a circle of stones, on the ground. Here the path decides to descend ten paces to the left before resuming its original course. You now head for trees, passing the prominent rowan tree on your right. The path continues, downhill, and reaches the tree line to finish, it would seem, in a fence which blocks your way. In fact it is simply sending you downhill to the left, winding an undulating course through trees to a stile and a road. *Quite a tricky piece of orienteering this, and I hope you got to the road OK.* Here you turn left.

8 Follow the road until you pass Shire Cottage on your right and then turn right. There's a waymark and a kissing gate to help you continue down along a footpath behind the house. Don't get too carried away by this path, because you are going to take a left hand-turn down through the wood, almost back on yourself. Find this path close to a house on stilts. You zigzag your way down through badger territory, out of the wood and into a field. Once there keep the hedge and ditch close by on your left. In the field corner find a stile, a waymark, a dinky little footbridge and a route across the next field. Make for a pronounced bridge over the river and through a gate. In this field go uphill, keeping the hedge to your left towards

habitation, noticing a waymark on a post confirming your route. You come to a stony field corner before following the field edge round, as it swings right to a gate and outbuildings. In the farmyard continue upwards, via a waymark on a post, and out through a gate, turning right along a driveway to reach a road.

9 When you reach the road proper, turn left and go uphill. *You have a good view of the way you have come, the rocky limestone outcrop dominating the landscape over to your left.* Ignore a road off to the left and continue uphill, quite steeply, past the house Llecha which is marked on the map. You are going to leave the road soon. Look out for a concrete driveway/track going off to the right and continue upwards along it, as concrete gives way to stone. Pass under power lines. Just as the stony track veers round you will join the North Wales Path and turn left onto it. The route, though, soon leaves the stony track, so keep your eyes open for a path going off to the left, through a kissing gate.

10 A delightful high-level stretch of walking evolves now, along the North Wales Path, clearly marked, as it winds its way through gorse and a kissing gate, providing enticing views over to the left. Another kissing gate brings you out onto a track where you turn right, to bear left at the fork, with houses, and join a road, keeping left to follow the waymark

Mochdre signed North Wales Path. Go downhill, with the chapel on the left, following the main, and noticeably broad, road round Llysfaen as it swings right past defunct toilets, and go down Dolwen

A547

18

Felin Mynydd

17

Road, leaving it to find Bwlch-y-Gwynt Road. Note a cautionary sign saying SLOW TOADS CROSSING (*presumably the fast toads have made it already*). Leave the road and follow The Lane off left, still on the North Wales Path. As you descend along the lane avoid the driveway to a house, choosing instead a gate to the right and a sign Public Footpath, past houses, through another kissing gate and down a track. At the bottom, by a small water trough, bear right downhill to a kissing gate. Go downhill between fences to another kissing gate. Up now through pleasant woodland and out again to cross a sloping field through gorse. Enter scrubland with blackthorn in blossom, violets underfoot and early bluebells, out of the wood and into another sloping field. *Woodland followed by field becomes quite a feature.* Make for a kissing gate on the far side and once again into woodland along a clear path, but pick out a somewhat damaged post with obliterated footpath sign guiding you off to the left. So don't go storming up the hill but follow this left-hand path, though not as far as the river, and leave woodland on the slope of the hill, rightish, heading for a field, keeping to the contours. You reach a kissing gate and go down a culvert into a field, skirting the hill. Follow the fence on the left as it works its way

16

Nant Ucha Farm

15

Cilgwyn-mawr **14** Meiofd

round, right and uphill to a golf course, of all things. *Before engaging golfers, we stopped for lunch.*

11 Continue uphill towards the golf course, looking out for stray golf balls (*we found one, well off target*). At the top, with views of the sea, turn left following the North Wales Path sign. Go down a lane, hedges to both sides until half way down you will come to a footpath sign off to the right. Go through a kissing gate and find yourself back on the golf course proper now. *Quite close to a green, too, so look out for approach shots.* Go downhill, seawards, making for a far corner, past

gorse and an oak tree then through a gate. Cross a track and reach a road, by the 6th Tee. But no time for golf, and anyway this is where you leave the North Wales Path, so turn left down the road.

12 You are among houses now, in Peulwys Lane. Change gear as you pass the 30 mph limit and travel up the other side. When you reach the main road, the B5383, turn left. Follow this for a short distance before climbing up Llanelian Road, as it branches off right. Quite a lengthy steep climb, this, as you look out for a footpath before you reach the top, well-signed, taking you thankfully off to the right.

13 Walk along a track here, level now, which becomes more of a lane fenced on both sides, with a good view of the extensive wind farm out at sea. Enter a field (*of horses, perhaps*) via a stile, and then cross in the same direction to the corner of a field where there is a stile.

65

Bear left at this, somewhat redundant, stile, keeping the hedge close on your left, following the field round to a corner and a stile. In the next field keep the hedge to your left to reach a corner and another stile, with a gate, onto a road. Turn right and go downhill, steeply to a bend, and in the dip turn left, as bidden by the walkers' sign, through a gate onto a track. Walk up to Meifod, with the stream on the left, gently up through trees. Pass the building, Meifod, over to the right, and where the path divides keep right via a stile and a consoling waymark. There is a deep stream to the left. *In fact the stream is probably shallow, but what I mean is it's a long way down.* A fence crosses your path, with a convenient low stile. Cross and continue in woodland edge, keeping the fence to your right. After a short distance go left to cross by a stile into an extensive field, where you turn sharp right, following the field edge close on your right to reach a stile. Once over the stile, with a crash landing in marshy territory, turn left and follow two field edges, first to a gate, then turning right, keeping the hedge close on your left to the field corner, where you will find a stile. Cross the next field, half left, making for houses on the skyline. A hedge crosses your path, but a footbridge and a stile help you through. Uphill now, make your way to the top, with a hedge on your left until you reach a stile propelling you onto a road. Turn right, facing the sea in the distance.

14 Follow the road to Cilgwyn-mawr. When you reach this farm you will see a waymark on a post in the field to your left. Use this to help you negotiate a detour round the property, coming out at the back of the farm through a kissing gate. Don't use the kissing gate opposite, but plunge down the tunnel-like lane, to your left, until you reach a place where three paths meet. Off to the left is a public footpath, and off to the right is another. But a stile leads you

downwards to skirt a property and bring you out onto a driveway, and then right, down to Cilgwyn Road.

15 Follow the road as it veers right and up to Nant Ucha Farm, turning right at the top. Soon after passing the buildings, look out for a bridle way going up, steeply, to the left. Don't get carried away, though, because with head down you might miss the footpath and stile off to the left, mercifully taking you back onto level territory.

16 Keeping the field edge to your left you might be surprised to see the unmistakable shape of Puffin Island and the edge of Anglesey in the sea ahead. A stile takes you to a lane going downhill to a kissing gate onto a road. Turn right. Cross to the other side of the road and turn left down a gully between houses and another kissing gate. A rather modest waymark on a slim post points you off left into a field. Go down the field along a well-mown, in our case, path to a gate and stile in the corner. Once in the field, make for a corner, half right where there is a gate and a stile enabling you to cross the next field to a gate and stile in the corner and access onto a minor road, where you turn left. Fields now give way to roads.

17 Follow the minor road now, downhill and over a river, keeping right at the road junction and through the 30 mph speed limit as you enter Mochdre, *where you encounter busy urban life again, after a whole day out in the country. You still have three miles to go to Conwy, though, and sadly, roads it has to be from Mochdre, as you have the dreaded A55 to by-pass again not to mention the urban sprawl of Llandudno Junction. And there is only one way to cross into Conwy.*

18 First of all in Mochdre you reach what looks like a crossroads on the map. Go straight on, and rightish, down an unnamed street towards the even busier Conway Road, and from here look for a road off to the left, Station Road. There's a row of shops on Conway Road and as you haven't passed a shop all day you may want to call in for provisions to fortify you on the last stage of your journey. Go down Station Road which straddles the A55, *of blessed memory*, and reach a T-junction where you turn left. You now have to follow a narrow, twisting road without a pavement, so beware traffic. After you pass a vineyard, *yes! a vineyard*, the road, which has now become Garth Road turns abruptly left and downhill to pass under the main road to Llandudno, high up on stilts above you. You reach Conway Road again, the A547, and there is no alternative but to use

it to pound your way through Llandudno Junction. So cross the busy road, turn right and follow the road round. *At least there is a pavement.* As you come to the end of the town, you need to find a route to the bridge crossing the river. We followed the main road, which goes right and then left to a roundabout. But there would seem to be another sneaky way of continuing down Conway road itself in its downgraded form. Whichever way you choose you need to cross the bridge over the river estuary on the right hand side, which is where the pavement is. Perversely you have to approach the bridge on the left-hand side and use a tunnel to switch lanes. Once on the bridge, forget your weariness and feast your eyes on the spectacular estuary, Telford's magnificent suspension bridge and, above all, the approaching towers of that most magnificent of castles, Conwy.

12 CONWY CASTLE to ABERGWYNGREGYN, castle site

Over wild uplands from Conwy, dip down to the sea once more, in your quest for the ancient capital of Glendower.

Distance: 15 miles
Gradient: One steep climb, ups and downs on top, ending along the sea edge
Terrain: Paths mostly, wild moorland, a little roadwork in the towns
Grade: Strenuous

If walking this section in a day, it is possible to park the car at Conwy, complete the walk and then catch the Llandudno bus back from Abergwyngregyn.

| Leaving the car in Benarth Road, Conwy, come out and turn right uphill under

the railway bridge, then through a narrow archway with Conwy Castle on the right. At the top turn right, following the main road and cross obediently via the pedestrian traffic lights. You can walk from here down to the quay, with Afon Conwy estuary to your right. *There are useful toilets here close to the Liverpool Arms.* Walk along the quayside past the 'Smallest House in Great Britain', out under an archway (*beware traffic*). Beyond you will see a walkers' sign for both the 'Wales Coast Path' and the 'North Wales Path', directing you off to the right to continue your journey along by the river, with good bird-spotting opportunities at low tide (*curlew, oystercatchers, waders*) on the approach to Bodlondeb Wood.

67

Conwy Castle

A World Heritage site, this outstanding and impregnable castle was built for Edward I between 1283 and 1287, on the site of first an Abbey and then Llywelyn the Great's fortification, standing proud on a narrow rocky outcrop close by the River Conwy, the river itself spanned by Telford's suspension bridge.

2 At the end of this pleasant waterside walk you reach a road, Morfa Drive, where walkers' signs direct you to turn sharp left, following the road past the school, Ysgol Aberconwy, to the main road, Bangor Road, which you cross. Ahead you will see the green footbridge over the railway line, which enables you to reach a small wall-lined path on woodland edge. Travelling uphill this path becomes Mountain Road, as you continue round and upwards, on tarmac now, (*with added traffic*). You come to a point where you need to leave the road and veer off upwards to the right onto a footpath, well-signed. So branch off up to the right into woodland,

and cross over a stile on your way up
Conwy Mountain. As you toil, spare a
moment to look back at the town, Conwy
Castle and the spectacular estuary.

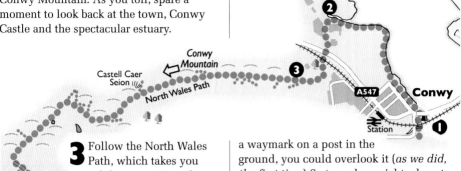

3 Follow the North Wales
Path, which takes you
round the mountain rather
than up to the summit.
*Where the path levels out
you reach a sign describing
Conwy Mountain Iron Age
Hill fort, Caer Seion, which
is up on the top to your
right. You may not have time
on this long walk for such a
diversion, though.* A little further
along there is a large stone block and a
sign indicating you have walked 2 miles
from Conwy and have 4 miles to walk to
Penmaenmawr (*though you're not actually
going there today*) Keep to the contours of
the hill. There are views beyond Conwy
now to the Great Orme above Llandudno.
Where a path crosses your route keep
on ahead through the bracken. The path
descends to join a farm track (*complete
with farmer on a tractor in our case*).
Follow the farm track which rounds the
hill and joins a road. You reach Bwlch
Sychnant; there is a car park here.

4 Cross the road and make your way
up to a metal gate between two
imposing pillars. Going through you enter
Pentrychnant Nature Reserve and pick up a
path with a stone wall on your left guarding
a plantation of trees. You are looking for
the North Wales Path now, which soon
arrives on your right but is easy to miss. It
is a sharp turn, right, and although there is

a waymark on a post in the
ground, you could overlook it (*as we did,
the first time*) So turn sharp right, almost
doubling up on yourself and go uphill on a
stony path. Another waymark, pointing left,
confirms your route, Follow a broad grassy
path, with sheep, passing under power
lines. Where the path divides follow The
North Wales Path to reach another parting
of the ways with a waymark. Go left here.
The North Wales Path is clear and well
marked throughout this section. Pass under
power lines again. Soon a wall comes in to
join you on your left, but the path shakes
it off and wanders to the right, seawards
and back under power lines here. You now
reach the top and are rewarded with good
views of Anglesey and Puffin Island ahead.
The path takes a leftish route, past a post
with waymark as you continue ahead, the
power lines a constant companion, now on
your left, quite a useful direction finder if
it's misty up here. Start a descent until you
come to a wall, with a gate and a ladder
stile which takes you just above the valley,
romantically named 'Fairy Glen'

5 The path now continues in a South
Westerly direction, maintaining
height round Maen Esgob and reaches a
wall, very stout and well-built. Keep the
wall on your right and follow it round.
Power lines are a useful indicator as you
negotiate the way round the contours of
the hill. The path goes upwards, passes
a large distinctive boulder and then

69

another, crosses a makeshift stream, and levels out. You should reach a prominent low level signpost before moving on to a deserted building shrouded in a few scant trees. Turn sharp right here and follow the wall down. *You have now joined The Pilgrim's Way.* The wall on your left comes to an end and you begin a descent down, leftish, through marshy ground to a stream which you cross by means of a footbridge.

A ladder stile just on the other side of the stream takes you into similar boggy territory as you forge your way upwards, and leftish via a foot-level post with waymark, under the familiar power lines to reach a black gate in a wall. Once through the gate you will discover a useful wayside map and reach a well-trodden track as you join the Wales Coast Path again. Turn left after the gate and keep the wall on your left.

6 The track enters land surrounding a house, Maen Crwn, through a black field gate taking you under fir trees with the house on your right. Just a little further distance on, the path decides to adopt a different direction (there is a waymark on a post), so strive right uphill to reach a gate and kissing gate in a wall. A little way beyond this, the path changes direction again and turns sharp left, well signed. You are walking upwards, though rounding the hill on your right. You reach the top, where, in good weather, you will see the sea, to the right, with Puffin Island off Anglesey very prominent. *Over to the left you will notice the stark outlines of the stone circle, well worth a visit, though only the Pilgrims Way path directs you to them.* Instead follow the directions to the right and a gradual

descent, picking up a wall on your right. You now come to a point where paths divide. The Pilgrims Way, which has completed its visit to the stone circle, and the North Wales Path

both go off left now into the valley of Nant-y-felin. However stay with the Wales Coast Path now, which makes its own way here to the right. There are waymarks. *Do not be tempted to go sharply uphill, to the right as if towards power lines.* Keep a more level path cross country.

7 Another foot-level waymark confirms the route. Round the hill, with more good views of Anglesey to the right, the path starts to descend, following a track. Pick up a wall on the left and follow it round under power lines to reach a gate. Once through the gate turn left on a well-used track downhill. Do not get carried away by this 'road' (*as we did*), because you need to find a path going off to the right. The beginning of this path is well signed, but the sign is not in a very useful position. You have to be almost on the path before you see it. This change is marked by a sudden left-hand bend in the road and a blank metal sign on the right. After you have successfully completed this change of direction, follow the path skirting the hill to your right, and descending as if towards the sea with a wall on your left. There is a gap in the wall. Directed by a walkers' sign in the ground, the path snakes its way down between gorse and bracken to pass under an oak tree where you branch off to the left. Notice a waymark. You reach a kissing gate by the side of a field gate where you enter a walled path, or narrow lane, which brings you to what is best described as a walkers' crossroads at the edge of buildings.

out via another kissing gate and onto a cul-de-sac road, named Gorwel. Turn left. Cross over to continue down Gorwel, pavements and houses to both sides, to reach another road at the bottom, Bryn Road where you turn right. Bryn Road becomes Village Road and you carry on down to the main road, Penmaenmawr Road, which you cross by means of the pedestrian traffic lights. Continue down Station Road, with Afon Llanfairfechan (*and useful public toilets*) on the left, before descending under the thunderous A55 and less thunderous railway line to come out onto the promenade, and an inviting café (*open nearly all the year round except in January*). Time for a cuppa.

9 Now focus your attention on the Wales Coastal Path again, walking into the setting sun (*if this is November*) The path is well marked, firm under foot and gives you a good chance to keep up your speed. Don't be surprised that at one stage the path

8 Here you will leave the Wales Coast Path to plunge down between buildings to find a descending public footpath. Where you have a choice between gaps in a wall, take the left-hand one to continue your more steep descent down a field to a kissing gate. From here bear left to go down a tarmac road. Just a little way on look out for a kissing gate on the right which takes you into a field. The path is hemmed in between a wall on the left and a fence on the right. As you reach the outlying houses of Llanfairfechan, go through another kissing gate and continue your way down. A slate path brings you

seems to want to go inland, before reforming itself and returning to the coast line. Your clear route passes nature reserves, over footbridges, at one stage even along the beach, through gates, before travelling over new walkways across Afon Aber to come out onto a road where there is a car park over to the right. Here turn left, and at this point you are going to leave the Wales Coast Path, as you make your way to Abergwyngregyn. So continue inland along the path which becomes a road, Station Road, avoiding the busy A55 by means of an underpass. Turn left after the tunnel to get to the village. The bus stop is on a wide turnaround section, to the left, and here you can catch your bus back to Conwy. A well-placed café lies across the road.

71

I 0 To visit the site of the former motte and bailey, which is on private land and can be seen but not reached, continue past the bus stop and just before the bridge over the river, pick up a footpath which will take you, via an information centre with toilets, into the village. The castle site is about as elusive as the scarlet pimpernel scattered along the roadside here. If you walk past the old post office and then left along the main road, you will see the mound appearing, apparently, in people's backyards. A rather disappointingly inaccessible relic of an illustrious past. However, you may want to take advantage of village facilities anyway: there are one or two cafés, or make your way back to the bus stop or car park.

I 3 ABERGWYNGREGYN to PENRHYN CASTLE

A leisurely stroll along the coast beside the swirling Menai Straits alive with birdlife, with fabulous views across to the island of Anglesey.

Distance: 5 miles
Gradient: Flat
Terrain: Coastal paths and some minor roadwork
Grade: Easy

If you park your car in Llandegai, you can catch one of the frequent buses to Abergwyngregyn and then walk back using this guide.

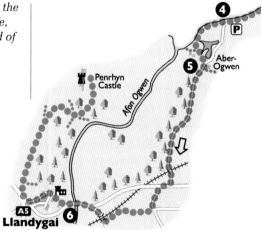

I Leave Abergwyngregyn from the bus stop, in its imposing turning area opposite the Aber Falls Café. Continue along the main road, as if towards Bangor. There is a handy pavement on the café side, which means you only have to cross the main road into Aber and not the very wide highway coming in from the A55. Follow the main road to Conwy, passing underneath the thundering A55, continuing left to reach a T-junction, where you leave the main route and turn right.

2 Follow this broad road down until it becomes narrower. After you pass houses on the right, the road divides. Take the left-hand option at the fork, pass under the railway bridge, over the cattle grid and rejoin the Wales Coast Path, which is well-marked with a signpost and many waymarks.

3 Go left at the signpost along a 'private road', which has a public right of way along it. After the property on the left the lane becomes more of a stony cart-track as you close in on the sea, with Anglesey prominent beyond. The cart-track comes to an end and you are directed onto the foreshore. This section is more unyielding underfoot, as you pick your way over pebbles and what are surely discarded flagstones. You might be tempted to try walking on the mud, if the tide is out, although remember it is mud. After a few hundred yards you are encouraged to go back onto dry land, which is a relief, so if you have been walking on the mudflats don't miss the waymark sign which shows you how to get back onto dry land. You now follow a grassy track, as Penrhyn Castle comes more prominently into view, to reach a point where a stream comes gushing out of two black pipelines. A path

marked 'HIDE' (*not an instruction*). Bearing right, not left unless you want to visit the hide, cleave your way through undergrowth to a gate where you turn left, through a gate marked Aber Ogwen and follow a path to the road. The path ends with a curious cantilever gate, onto a road. Turn right. *Some road work follows.*

also joins you here, from the left. Continue ahead along the coast path to pass through a small copse of trees, good cover to watch waders on the estuary (*birds*) and beyond this feature a kissing gate taking you onto a path now quite distinctly in a field. You are walking with fences on both sides, as Snowdon appears prominently on your left. A gate, with no fastening and a waymark is followed by a gate complete with fastening. Here there is an alternative path off left, but carry on ahead along the Wales Coast Path to another kissing gate, with a waymark. This takes you out of the field onto a path under trees, down some steps onto the foreshore again for a short distance before entering a car park, on your left. The car park has picnic tables and information panels, *but not an ice cream van, which would have been welcome on this hot summer afternoon.*

4 Leave the car park by continuing along the coast, even though the waymark invites you to take the road. There is another public footpath which leads back onto the beach for a short while, as you keep Penrhyn Castle in your sights. Soon after the gaunt wooden stilts on the beach you pass a wooden bird hide on the left and immediately plunge into woodland, left,

5 So follow the narrow road, which has considerable traffic. The hedge on the right becomes a stone wall, before the road crosses over the railway line via a bridge. You come to a main road, where your turn right at the T-junction. Follow the main road for a very short distance before leaving it, left, to take a subsidiary road, marked 'Tal-y-bont'. This road has a pavement for a short distance, before shedding it. You are now following signs indicating 'The Wales Coast Path' again. You reach a junction of paths, with a plethora of signs, and you go right, through a kissing gate to pick up a footpath by the side of the church, which is on your left, with a wooden fence on the right. Another kissing gate brings you into a field. Keeping the open field on your right and hedge on your left make for a field corner, and beyond that a clump of trees. You now have trees on your left and a wire fence guarding you from the railway line on the right. Another kissing gate. *This section of the walk was completed during hurricane Ophelia, so there is more wind than voice in my voice recorder, not to mention the OS map unfurling itself, deliberately in my opinion, so some of these instructions are a little unclear. I hope it all makes sense.* The path slopes down, a fence on either side, with the railway line now higher than you are to bring you out on a road with a waymark sign, indicating you turn right to go under the railway bridge.

6 This road, without a pavement, brings you back to the main road with a pavement. Turn left onto the main road and progress uphill. Once past the impressive stone entrance on the right cross over to the pavement on the other side, and this will take you over the broad river Ogwen, alive with wildlife. Soon after passing a wall-mounted fountain, look for a stone arch to

go through, and turn right off the main road through the gate and up the tarmac path the other side, a stone wall now on the left. When you reach the top you come to a kind of crossroads, the church on the right. Take the road almost directly opposite, keeping No 10 on your left. When you come to a fork take the major road off to the left, and this will bring you to the main road, and the entrance to Penrhyn, looking more like a prison than a castle, but there you are. *The castle is a National Trust property and their rules apply, if you want to visit.*

14 PENRHYN CASTLE to BEAUMARIS CASTLE, Anglesey

A coastal exploration, crossing onto Anglesey along Telford's superb suspension bridge, as you make your way to that most westerly outpost, Beaumaris Castle.

Distance: 9 miles
Gradient: Mostly sea level, a little uphill work on Anglesey
Terrain: Footpaths and minor roads with a pavement stretch along the A5
Overall: Easy

Llandygai is a useful starting point for both this walk and Walk 15. Leave your car opposite the bus stop and catch buses back after the walk is over. Buses back to Bangor leave from outside the Bakery in Castle Street, Beaumaris, and are fairly regular, taking you on a long and circuitous route via the hospital, and other highlights of the town to the bus station where you can pick up a bus, destined for Llandudno or Bethesda, back to Penrhyn Castle and your waiting car.

1 Leave the forbidding entrance to Penrhyn Castle at Llandygai and cross the main road, to take a minor (unnamed)

road, marked 'Rugby Ground', and use the right-hand pavement. At a road junction, turn right, noticing the 'Wales Coast Path' sign and proceed uphill for a little way by the side of the road. Not far up here there is a cunning footpath, off to the right, which will bring you out onto the A5, heavy with traffic. Cross the A5 with care to pick up a footpath, signed with a fingerpost, on the other side by means of a kissing gate. Walk along a path with fences on both sides. Over to the right is a prominent air shaft. You pass woodland on the right before the path ends at a minor road.

2 Cross and go through another kissing gate into a field. Keeping woodland to the left, at the end of the field you cross a track and pick up another path between two sets of metal fences. On the left, down below, is the railway line. The path ends at a road, where you turn left into an industrial site and go down hill. Where the road swings round to the right carry on ahead to a barrier across this wide tarmac road. Beyond the barrier you will come to the old railway line, where you turn right.

74

Penrhyn Castle

The current 'castle' was designed by Thomas Hopper and built
in neo-Norman style between 1820 and 1833.

3 Keeping the river on your left you follow the old railway line down to the port. You pass under the road bridge and reach the water. Turn sharp left and go uphill to the road, possibly meeting heavy traffic. You come to the main road, the A5, where you turn right. Follow the A5 for a short distance, on the pavement. Good views over to the right of the bay and the Straits. You come to the Lord Nelson pub on the left. Here a sign on an electricity lamp standard directs you off the road into a car park. Keep close to the blue railings on the right. When you reach a white metal gate and road system, turn right, through the new housing development. Keep the new houses on the left and go uphill towards the older houses. At the top here, turn right, on the pavement with good views of the mountains beyond the bay, and this road takes you down to Bangor Pier, which you can stroll along if you wish (entrance charge) There are also toilets here.

4 After the pier go up through the gardens back to a road, Ffordd Siliwen, a hotel facing you, and then turn right onto the road, which you follow, as it continues uphill, with yellow lines on both sides. *There are choices here, depending on the tide levels. It is possible to take a path down and walk along the shore line, but only if the tide is receding or out, and perversely you may not know this until you have made the decision! So if you are unsure, consult the local tide tables.* If you do take this option, choose the second path down from the Ffordd Siliwen, *which is unmarked – it's just before lamppost 28, if that's any help.* Go downhill here through woodland. The path is steep and narrows as it reaches the shore line. A path comes in via a black gate on the left, but carry on down until you reach the shore line. If all is well, you can then take this short but interesting detour along the shore. You will reach a concrete driveway* (*and a walker's*

Beaumaris Castle

sign telling you you have walked the shore line route).

5 To follow the safer route, continue along Ffordd Siliwen which becomes Ffordd Menai before taking the second road off to the right, Ffordd Gorad where you will rejoin the coastal path, at * above.

6 Cross the driveway and go into a field to the right of another concrete driveway through a gate. Keep the fence on your right and go uphill into trees where you will find a gate taking you into Nant-porth Nature Reserve. This pleasant woodland walk goes up via steps to a barn-like structure, where you leave the Nature Reserve and continue through a gate between two fences, woodland on the right and field on the left. After you have steered your way round the fields, you will come out onto a tarmac path by the football ground turn left and go uphill. Keep the football complex on the right, the right veers round to come out at the entrance to Bangor City football ground and a roundabout on the A5, again.

7 Turn right here and follow the A5 for a fair distance to the bridge over the Menai Straits. Approaching Telford's bridge be prepared to leave the Wales Coast Path, as it disappears on its way south, and instead cross over the spectacular bridge to Anglesey. After a high level walk along Telford's spectacular bridge, you set foot on Ynys Mon

8 On the right is the aptly named Bridge Inn, where you turn sharp right down Cambria Road, Ffordd Cambria. Follow the road through the No Entry sign and look out for a footpath sign on a post taking you off right down some steps. You now reach a minor road, Water Street, where you turn left. Follow the road, as another, Fairview, comes in from the left where there are some useful toilets. Keep going, with Prince's Pier off to

Chicle Hill

A545

Menai Strait

Ynys Gaint

9

St George's Road

Ynys Faelog

7

8
Menai
Suspension
Bridge

A5

the right. When you get to the Liverpool Arms turn sharp right down St George's Road and after a few yards go onto the pier complex, eventually leaving it to regain the road, turning right at the walkers' sign. Continue along St George's

Road, with Askew Street coming in from the left, to veer up to the left at Menai Ville Terrace. Keep right on to the end of the road where you reach Cadnant Road, the main road out of Menai Bridge, and here you turn right.

9 *A considerable stretch of road walking follows, but there is a pavement.* Just before you come to the 40 mph sign take the road left, Cichle Hill, and follow this steep hill upwards and round,

skirting Llandegfan. The pavement runs out on the right and then vanishes altogether, as superb views of Snowdonia open up, to the right. You come to the end of the speed limit and carry on. The road narrows, with less traffic, and where it veers left, look out for a signed path going off to the right, over the stone stile into the field. *You are now in the countryside again.*

BEAUMARIS

10 The path crosses a boggy section before turning a corner where you can see a sign on a post over to the left. Make for this yellow-hatted post and enter woodland. Follow the well-marked and well-trodden path through woodland and scrub to another gate. Improved duckboarding over a muddy patch leads to a kissing gate into woodland and a change of direction, veering right. Another kissing gate takes you into a well cut field which turns out to be a lawn. We are now at Pen y Parc and from here walk down their drive, with a sign on a post hidden under fuchsia.

11 Where the drive forks, take the right hand version to the road, which you follow, keeping right. A golf course looms into view. Continue along the road, past the entrance to the golf club, on your left, down the steep hill with wonderful views of Beaumaris, the mountains beyond the Menai Straits. You come to the main road, where you turn left and walk into the town of Beaumaris and its castle, visible from the town centre.

15 PENRHYN CASTLE to DOLBADARN CASTLE

From the coast take the historic slate trail along the old railway line to reach the mountains at last and Dolbadarn Castle at the foot of mighty Snowdon.

Distance: 10 miles
Gradient: A gradual climb into Snowdonia
Terrain: After the old railway line becoming more open and uneven moorland
Level: Moderate

1 Leave the forbidding entrance to Penrhyn Castle at Llandygai and cross the main road, to take a minor (unnamed) road, marked 'Rugby Ground'. Use the right-hand pavement. At a road junction, turn right, noticing the 'Wales Coast Path' sign and proceed uphill for a little way by the side of the road. Not far up here there is a cunning footpath, off to the right, which will bring you out onto the A5, heavy with traffic. Cross the A5 with care to pick up a footpath, signed with a fingerpost, on the other side by means of a kissing gate. Walk along a path with fences on both sides. Over to the right is a prominent Air Shaft. You pass woodland on the right before the path ends at a minor road, where you leave it via a kissing gate and turn left.

2 Follow this road, now signed 'Snowdonia Slate Trail', and continue gradually downhill, passing woodland on the right. There soon appears a misleading waymark sign on a post suggesting you should branch off left along a spanking new wide gravel path. Inviting though this may be it leads nowhere, so harden your heart and leave it alone, carrying on down the road. Go over a Railway bridge and dip down to a ford. Just before the ford, turn

off left to join the old slate quarry railway line, where you turn right. There's a useful information board here telling you about the Cegin Valley, which you now enter.

3 There follows a lengthy and pleasant stretch along the tarmac surface of a cycle path through trees close to the river (Afon Cegin) on your right. Gates take you in and out of a short stretch of genuine roadway, allowing you to pass underneath the snarling A55. Turn left again and you are back onto the reclaimed cycleway, now gifted with a name, Lôn Ogwen. Walk on over the long walled bridge to reach a prominent new green bridge over the A4244, with glimpses of steam railway paraphernalia over to your left. This walkway takes you under first one bridge and then another, before going uphill to pass a house on the left and a tempting footpath, to be ignored, on your right. As you approach the next bridge, the main route dips down underneath it, but here you need to take the subsidiary path, left, guiding you through a walkers' gate. Turn right here and cross the bridge spanning the way you came.

4 Once over the bridge you need to look out for a subtle change of direction. You leave the path, which swings sharply round to the left, but your route lies directly ahead. To do this, perversely, go through a walkers' gate, right, and immediately over a ladder stile, left, which will take you into a field. Now continue on a track as it winds its way gradually up, with field edge and stream to your right. You pass interesting wooden buildings and a smallholding on your left, before turning right through an

78

open gateway to reach inhabited buildings on your left, with a waymark. Turn right here, keeping an uninhabited building on your left, pass a small waterfall and go through a kissing gate, with a waymark on the post, left, and into a field.

5 You need to follow a rough path keeping hawthorn and other trees on your left on a sort of low ridge with bluebells (in season). The countryside seems more open at this point, but make for woodland ahead, ignoring a path crossing the one you are on. Don't go uphill. There is a prominent wooden structure, which could have all sorts of uses, on your right, and a post in the ground labelled Number 5 on your left, just before you plunge into woodland through a walkers' gate. Follow the path for a short distance before finding a sturdy gate which gives access into managed woodland.

6 Go uphill now through this attractive woodland edge, using another gate into gorse, ignoring a path off to the left, continuing more uphill. You reach a ladder stile and beyond that a somewhat redundant gate, before bearing left to reach a kissing gate which gives access onto a lane. Turn right on the lane. Where the lane forks go left and continue upwards, but keep a sharp lookout for your next manoeuvre. It's tempting to carry straight on, but there is a subtle path off left, waymarked, which takes you deep into the pine forest. This path, with a stream in it, continues upwards with traces of wall on both sides until you reach a T-junction of paths, where you turn right. (There is a waymark on a tree).

7 Your path between gloomy pine trees is joined by a wall coming in from the left before you eventually reach a gate. Do not use the gate. Instead turn left, through a gap in the wall. Once you have taken this turn,

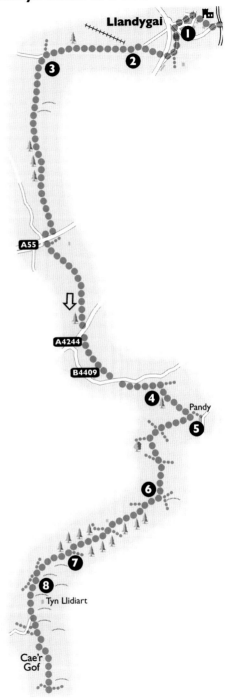

go upwards through mixed woodland to come out by way of a kissing gate. Continue along here, between a steep hillside with bilberries coming down on your left and a wall on your right, until your path opens out. Views of the coastline emerge now on your right, as the stony path takes you under power lines to reach a gate in a wall and a good stop for your packed lunch. Go through the gate, turning left in the walled lane.

8 Go uphill to reach the house, Tyn Llidiart, and immediately descend along a metalled road to the right, with good views continuing over on your right. But keep a sharp look out for a footpath, and signpost, on your left through a kissing gate to follow a farm track towards Cae'r Gof. Pass these farm buildings on your right and continue ahead on the level (with a waymark on a post) to find a rough cart track taking you out into more open country. You reach a gate and a kissing gate, rather detached, in the wall to the left, to pick up this rough cart track again as it continues through a gap in the wall. Where paths diverge go ahead, with a building to the left, and on through another gap in a wall and another. However, after this wall there is a subtle change of direction.

9 Go uphill here, half left to an exit point which you can't see. As you climb further uphill, a waymark on a post appears and a hidden gate in the wall ahead, hidden, because it's sideways on and you may not see it before you reach it! Turn right here onto common land. Continue now with the wall on your right, gradually descending, realising you seem to be making a detour, which in fact you are. In the next field corner there is a walkers' gate. Go through here into quite different territory. You face rough and boggy terrain as you descend half left. I imagine this section would be hard work in wet weather

and difficult to navigate in mist. There are marker posts (one uprooted) which help you maintain a direct line to reach a gully, a stream, a wall and trees. This is one of those occasions when you will know you have arrived when you reach it, but it may be baffling to find in difficult circumstances.

10 Once up from the gully, skirt round the hill over to your left for a while. More posts keep you close to the wall on your right through a broken wall to reach another marker post urging you to change direction, left. Here you go stoutly uphill, aiming for the deserted ruin. Go to the right of the ruin and immediately turn left, through a gate, keeping the wall on your left for a short distance before following the path more uphill, striking across moorland. The terrain changes again, as you walk through heather and bilberries and bracken, hill-walking now, aiming as if for a prominent high ridge in the distance, always following the distinctive, if wayward, path upwards. As you reach the crest, the magnificent peak of Snowdon appears ahead, seen from an untypical viewpoint but unmistakeable, if the weather is kind.

11 Soon you reach a kissing gate in a wall and begin the descent, keeping close to the wall on your right to find another hidden sideways gate in the field corner. In this next field keep the wall to your right and continue downhill between two low walls to reach a wooden gate which takes you suddenly out of the countryside and into the back yard of a house. Keep this house to your right and look out for a way leading off the drive, right, to follow a secluded path (with a waymark) to reach a kissing gate providing access onto a main road where you turn right.

12 Continue along this main road, looking out for the second footpath off to the left through a kissing gate and onto a bridle path, taking you towards habitation, another kissing gate and a rapid descent into the village of Deiniolen, where you turn left onto High Street. Almost immediately (past the Bull public house) you turn right into New Street, passing a shop on the right where you can top up supplies before turning left into a street, Tai Caradog. Continue along this street, turning right at the end through a kissing gate, descending to reach two footbridges over a stream, before going up again to reach a kissing gate onto a lane where you turn left. Almost at once turn right off the lane, to find a footpath and a kissing gate which gives access onto rough land with an uneven surface. The only way now is up. At the fork, the path narrows and climbs between walls to reach a house. Go through the gate here and continue upwards along the driveway to the road, where you turn left, on your way to Maes Eilian.

13 Follow the road for a while, going right where it joins another road. You reach houses on the left and a bus shelter appears on your right. Llanberis Lake is now very prominent, over to the right. Just before the bus shelter there is a kissing gate and footpath descending, with steps, and this is your route. Go down to a lane, cross it and find another footpath opposite, between buildings, turning right just beyond, onto an access road. As this road takes a sharp turn to the right, go left instead, through a gate and into woodland. There follows a pleasant walk over a metal bridge and via a kissing gate through into Padarn Country Park. A long descent follows through woodland and slate, slippery underfoot at times, as you make your way downwards along the many paths to the old hospital and the Quarry Museum at the foot. You may have time to visit the

Quarry Museum (*though it closes at 17.00*). To reach Dolbadarn Castle, make initially for the large car park. On the other side of the main road, there is a footpath to the castle. Go down some slate steps and cross the footbridge over the stream to a kissing gate on the other side and carry on upwards, bearing left at the sign. The castle soon comes into view. Pass a stone shack, go through a kissing gate and continue up to view the Round Tower of Dolbadarn Castle, *open all the year round.*

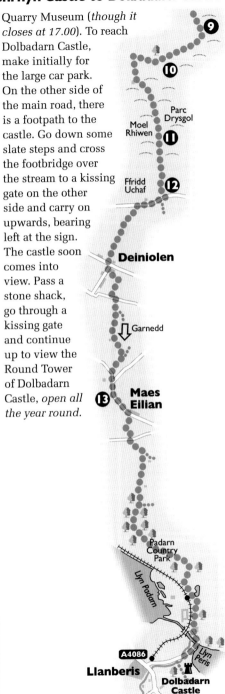

81

16 DOLBADARN CASTLE (Llanberis) to DOLWYDDELAN CASTLE

Dolbadarn Castle

Built by Llywelyn the Great in the 13th century this mountain castle at the foot of Snowdon became the notorious 20 year prison of Llywelyn ap Gruffud's brother Owain.

A spectacular mountain walk through the heart of Snowdonia.

Distance: 15 miles (not including Snowdon)
Gradient: One harsh climb up the road via the Llanberis Pass, and another steep climb up to Bwlch y Rhediad

Terrain: Main road (5 miles), stony path, upland tracks and paths
Rating: Strenuous

There are two ways of completing this walk: **The more direct route** *along the road from Llanberis to Pen-y-Pass, and on to*

Dolwyddelan. Distance 15 miles
The more daunting, though rewarding,
route from Llanberis via SNOWDON to
Pen-y-Pass, and from there to Dolwyddelan.
Allow an extra 6-7 hours for the climb up
Snowdon and descent to Pen-y-Pass.

The pros and cons of both routes:

ROUTE 1: by road via the LLANBERIS
PASS
• *the shorter route enabling you to*
complete the walk from castle to castle in
one day.
• *a long and unrewarding trudge up the*
main road for 5 miles. (2 hours of tedium)
If you are not too much of a purist, as a
walker, there are two ways to avoid this
hostile climb by road, either by using the
service bus from Llanberis to Pen-y-Pass or
by taking one of the numerous taxis plying
their trade up from Llanberis.

On the day we walked I counted 165
cars coming towards me between Nant
Peris and Pen y Pass. It's sheer drudgery
and took us 2 hours from Llanberis.

By the way, if ever you are thinking of
parking the car at Pen-y-Pass, note that this
car park soon reaches capacity, particularly
summer time weekends. (£5 for 4 hours,
current rates, and £10 a day). The car park
at Dolwyddelan is close to the castle, and
is free. Note that Dolbadarn Castle is free
to enter, and open all the year round, while
Dolwyddelan Castle charges for entry and
has specific opening times. Check details
before you set out, if you want to visit.

ROUTE 2: via SNOWDON

• *a good chance to take in the highest*
mountain in England and Wales as part of
a linear walk.
• *tough conditions, and in any case you*
would have to accept being unable to do
the whole walk from castle to castle in a
single day.

ROUTE I STAGE ONE:
DOLBADARN CASTLE TO
PEN-Y-PASS by road.

Allow 2 hours to walk to Pen-y-Pass from
Dolbadarn. Park your car in the convenient
Dolbadarn car park (£4 current prices).
Note 'gates close at 8pm' However there
were 'no gates' on the day we travelled,
though perhaps they intend to install them,
and we came back to find the car accessible
after 8pm. We averaged 2 miles an hour
walking, so with stops for breaks and
navigation and the return trip by car we
took 10 hours. You will probably take less,
but it's as well to allocate a good amount
of time. Our trip was on a glorious summer
day with wall to wall sunshine. That's
not always the case in Snowdonia. You
can reach Llanberis from Dolwyddelan by
bus, or train and bus, but we walked on a
Sunday and bus times were not convenient,
so we did the two car trick.

I Leave the Dolbadarn car park and find
the start of the walk on the opposite side
of the main road. Go down some slate steps
and cross the footbridge over the stream to
a kissing gate on the other side and carry on
upwards, bearing left at the sign. The castle
soon comes into view. Pass a stone shack,
go through a kissing gate and continue up
to view the Round Tower of Dolbadarn
castle.

2 Leave the castle surroundings via a
different route, left of the path you
came up on, plunging down between
bracken and silver birches. The path then
forks. Go left, downhill. The path opens
out to a kissing gate and a small car park
beyond. Up from here you will reach the
main road where you turn left to find a
pavement. The lake comes into view, on
your left, with the impressive slate of the
Electric Mountain behind it, and go past
the speed limit sign. You come to the head

83

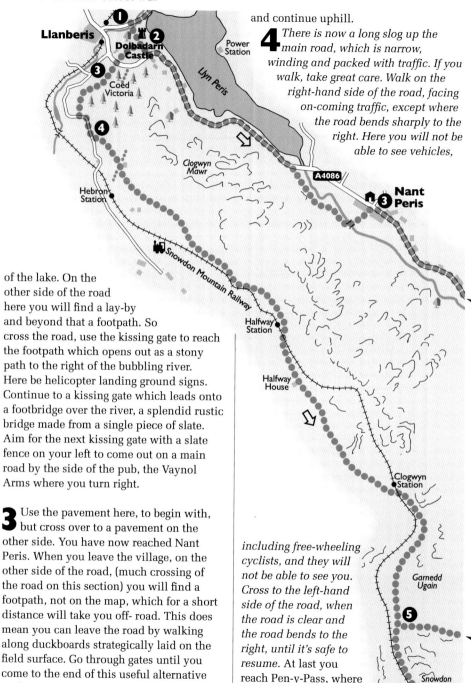

and continue uphill.

4 *There is now a long slog up the main road, which is narrow, winding and packed with traffic. If you walk, take great care. Walk on the right-hand side of the road, facing on-coming traffic, except where the road bends sharply to the right. Here you will not be able to see vehicles,*

of the lake. On the other side of the road here you will find a lay-by and beyond that a footpath. So cross the road, use the kissing gate to reach the footpath which opens out as a stony path to the right of the bubbling river. Here be helicopter landing ground signs. Continue to a kissing gate which leads onto a footbridge over the river, a splendid rustic bridge made from a single piece of slate. Aim for the next kissing gate with a slate fence on your left to come out on a main road by the side of the pub, the Vaynol Arms where you turn right.

3 Use the pavement here, to begin with, but cross over to a pavement on the other side. You have now reached Nant Peris. When you leave the village, on the other side of the road, (much crossing of the road on this section) you will find a footpath, not on the map, which for a short distance will take you off- road. This does mean you can leave the road by walking along duckboards strategically laid on the field surface. Go through gates until you come to the end of this useful alternative surface and reach the road again. Turn right

including free-wheeling cyclists, and they will not be able to see you. Cross to the left-hand side of the road, when the road is clear and the road bends to the right, until it's safe to resume. At last you reach Pen-y-Pass, where there is a welcome café and toilets.

ROUTE 2 STAGE ONE:
DOLBADARN CASTLE TO
PEN-Y-PASS via SNOWDON

This is by far the most spectacular route from Dolbadarn to Pen-y-pass, but the time needed (allow 6 hours, though it took me 7) means that you would be most unlikely to complete the whole walk to Dolwyddelan in one day. Though using the train up Snowdon and walking down to Pen-y-Pass might make it possible. However there is a good bus service from Pen-y-Pass back to Llanberis (we caught one at 1805). You could also stay in the YHA at Pen-y-Pass and complete the walk the following day. It's worth bearing in mind that

Snowdon is a long, hard climb, and you should not underestimate the difficulty of navigation if cloud is low. Also take into account the low temperature, even in high summer. We walked over the August Bank Holiday, when, with the wind chill factor, the temperature on the summit was 5°. Well prepared walkers were wearing boots, anoraks, hats and even gloves. And this was August!

I Leave the Dolbadarn car park and find the start of the walk on the opposite side of the main road. Go down some slate steps and cross the footbridge over the stream to a kissing gate on the other side and carry on upwards, bearing left at the sign. The castle soon comes into view. Pass a stone shack, go through a kissing gate and continue up to view the Round Tower of Dolbadarn castle.

2 From the castle, walk down towards the wood, but not back the way you came from the car park. There is a path down from the ruin which passes through a sort of fence, more like disconnected concrete fence posts. This will take you into silver

birch woodland. Very soon you reach a junction of paths. There are three ways you could go, so walk straight across, to travel in a southerly direction. You join another path where you turn left, a private

85

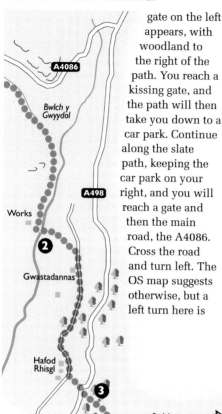

gate on the left appears, with woodland to the right of the path. You reach a kissing gate, and the path will then take you down to a car park. Continue along the slate path, keeping the car park on your right, and you will reach a gate and then the main road, the A4086. Cross the road and turn left. The OS map suggests otherwise, but a left turn here is

road, where you turn left.

4 You are now on the acknowledged trek up Snowdon, as the road goes steeply upwards. Not far along the road you will see the footpath, the Llanberis path, signed off to the left. Go through the gate with its prominent sign 'Path to Snowdon summit' and you are on the mountain proper. *You will probably not need any more directions from me, as you simply join the throng of people, like pilgrims, making their way up to the top. It's no exaggeration to say that the day we walked we probably encountered 500 people on the same trail.* The path follows its steady course upwards, occasionally close to the railway line and its chuntering trains, and on a couple of occasions goes under the railway line. You reach the Halfway House, a welcome stop, complete with refreshments, before resuming the climb.

5 A route marker to look out for, as you reach the crest of the Horseshoe, is a stone pillar on the left*, marking the beginning of your

correct.

3 Almost immediately leave the main road, right, crossing into woodland via a ladder stile. Follow the broad track through woodland, Coed Victoria, or Victoria Wood as she translates into English. The broad track veers round and you reach a gate, with a waymark on a tree directing you right. This stony path becomes narrower as it winds its way among the trees and through a kissing gate. You emerge out of woodland through a gate with a house to the left and into a yard. From here it is but a step onto a minor

descent to Pen-y-Pass. At the moment, however, you will be heading for the summit, so battle on to the top. You may be in cloud when you get there, and also find you have to join a queue to climb up to the trig point! But there's still a great sense of achievement, to have walked to the top of the highest mountain in England and Wales. *Tucked in close by is the café. You have to admit that Snowdon is well endowed with cafés.* And then for the descent. Retrace your steps to the stone pillar* and follow the way down on the pathway to your right. This is a much more uneven path, at times helped by boulders which have been airlifted in to create a substantial route, *though my suspicion is they are more helpful on the way up than on the way down, which is often marked by changes in levels, patches of scree and streams crossing.* A choice has to be made between using the Pyg track and the Miners track, and this is the one we followed. It certainly provides more level sections. You are making first for Glaslyn, the lake cradled in Snowdon's arms.

6 Once you reach the lake you are lulled into a false sense of security as the path levels out, only to plunge downwards again to the next sheet of water, the reservoir, Llyn Llydaw. Now you're shaping, and can increase your pace, which you might need to do if you're trying to catch a bus – there's still a mile to march to Pen-y-pass. But soon you round a bend, see the road, then the hostel and finally the car park where the bus turns. *You've made it!*

**BOTH ROUTES STAGE THREE:
PEN-Y-PASS to DOLWYDDELAN**

1 At Pen-y-Pass cross the car park entrance to a kissing gate

and descend the mountain, the main road rapidly disappearing to your left, as you follow rough stone steps down into the valley. The path is fairly steep. You reach a footpath sign, where paths divide. Go right. Continue your descent. You come to a section where they are resurfacing the footpath with rocks which seem to have

fallen from the sky in black bags. *As you prepare to cross a rushing stream you will notice on the map that paths diverge. But be warned. This is a clear case of a path on the map having no resemblance to a path on the ground.* So, do not go left, but instead follow the direction of the waymark on a post directing you over a footbridge. On the other side the new stone path gives way to a more gravelly, but clear path downhill. As you round the corner you will see the Water Works (Works on the map) nestling, (if water works can nestle) among fir trees. You reach a walkers' gate, turn left on the access road and go through more splendid gates to the Works.

2 Once through the gates, stay with the access road upwards, to join a path coming in from the left and here you turn right. Cross a stream, and follow a broad track with stone walls to each side. Further along there is a gate across the road, a house to the right, and a cattle grid. Continue along the road. Ignore a small galvanised gate off to the left. Instead, a little further along, as

the road goes over a stream find a gate beyond, on your left. *According to the map the footpath should leave the road before the stream, but it doesn't.* Go through the gate, off left, beyond the stream with a sign which announces, somewhat bizarrely, 'Wirral Grammar School for Girls' (*oddly this sign was missing, the second time we came. Was this uprooted by the hurricane, or did I imagine it all.....?*) Go up the steep field from here to reach a main road via a prominent ladder stile. With good views of the Snowdon Horseshoe this is a good spot for lunch, if you can get off the road.

3 On the other side of the road is a kissing gate, enabling you to reach open country beyond. A Bridle Way fingerpost sign here points, rather unhelpfully, to the right. However you need to go straight up the mountain side. *Perhaps horses will take more of a zigzag route, but we never found out.* So, instead, like horses, take the bit between your teeth and mount the more vertical route up towards a yellow walkers' sign in front of woodland. *Not really vertical, by the way, it just feels like that.* As you climb higher, incidentally, more of the Snowdon range comes into view behind you, so take breathers and look across at that most magnificent mountain range. There are several waymarks to help, as you climb upwards, the path following the course of a stream, which could prove hazardous in very wet weather. Beyond the tree line, good views emerge of the lake, Llyn Gwynant below the dominant Snowdon Horseshoe. The footpath takes a bit of a right-hand squiggle, but still ascends as you reach open territory with boulders and bracken. And you reach the top at a ladder stile over a wall and a kissing gate. What a view!

4 Now for the descent, which is gentler. After a ladder stile aim for a point to the right of trees along a path well-marked. *However there is much deforestation going on here, and the trees might have gone by now.* Look out for a low ruined building on your right-hand side with a copse of trees below. Here you need to leave the path you are on, turn right, and find or make a path between the copse of trees on your right and a stream on your left. Go downhill in this fashion. A path does seem to emerge as you close in on the trees, but you may still have to make your own way. Cross the stream on your left to a prominent waymark post. Your objective is a broad

footbridge over another rushing stream.

5 Use the footbridge and go up the other side to a gate and a very good stile over the fence. The path now follows the contours of the hill, often doubling up as a stream. It can be marshy here. You will reach a gate, where we saw a modern-day shepherd on a quad bike, one of very few humans encountered on the way from Pen-y-Pass. The path descends, more steeply down now, to a farm, and you are off the mountain, finding yourself in a farmyard with dogs and hens. Turn left along the access road.

6 This road brings you down to a T-junction, where you turn left along a minor road which you follow, crossing a river. You reach a house, left, Ffrith, as the road bends sharply to the right bedecked with fantastic rose-bay willow herb. Where the road turns sharply to the right, leave it (there is a walkers' sign attached to a gate) and look out for a path through the farmyard which leads you up to a field gate, with a ladder stile to the left. You are now in fields. You face another gate, with a ladder stile to the right, travelling uphill a bit. Where the path divides take the right-hand fork to a gate, with a waymark on as post. Here there is another path going off to the right, which according to the map should take you to the castle, but a more distinct route lies ahead, so take this direct option, along a rutted track. Once over the brow look ahead and there you will see Dolwyddelan Castle. A gate crosses the path and the end of your day's walk is in sight. You actually go past the castle, on your right, and pick up a downhill tarmac track. Look out for a path which leaves the road on your right, and this will take you down to buildings which turn out to be toilets and the entrance house to the castle where you can buy tickets for entry. Leaving here, downhill, you will reach a

17 DOLWYDDELAN CASTLE to CASTELL TOMEN-Y-MUR

Dolwyddelan Castle

Built by Llewelyn the Great in the early 13th century, this mountain castle controlling the approaches to Snowdonia via the Vale of Conwy was captured, strengthened and extended by Edward I in 1283, before its inevitable decline.

Over the Crimea Pass to the slate town of Blaenau Ffestiniog before river crossings on your way to a long-forgotten Roman encampment and the desolate high land above Trawsfynydd.

Distance: 15 miles
Gradient: Two steep climbs
Terrain: Some road work, but mostly footpaths
Level: Strenuous

The main difficulty with this part of walk lies in choosing how to get from the starting point, Dolwyddelan Castle, to the slate town of Blaenau Ffestiniog, en route to Castell Tomen-y-mur.

The problem is the main road between Dolwyddelan up to the Crimea Pass and down into Blaenau Ffestiniog. Try as I might I cannot find a reasonable walk up to the Crimea Pass. The best route, on paper, would seem to be to walk to Hendre, cross under the railway line and then strike up to join a track which comes out at the top of the pass. Unfortunately there is no discernible path, and certainly no waymarks. I cannot recommend this route, struggling, as I did, to clamber up through hostile terrain, at one point only managing ¼ mile in one hour. So I suggest one of the following routes, though your choice may be affected by the way you are operating. If you are doing this as a day's walk and want to avoid the Crimea Pass and are based in Dolwyddelan or close to the castle, choose ROUTE 1. If based in Trawsfynydd, choose ROUTE 2. If you are happy to walk by road up to the Crimea Pass, choose ROUTE 3.

ROUTE I

Avoid walking the main road over the Crimea Pass by catching a bus, or even a train from Dolwyddelan to Blaenau Ffestiniog. Pick up the walk as described below in ROUTE 3 (point 5) in the town, walk to Castell Tomen y Mur and then on to Trawsfynnyd where you can catch buses back to Dolwyddelan.

ROUTE 2

Catch the 0808 bus from Trawsfynydd to Blaenau Ffestiniog, and walk back to Trawsfynydd from there. Follow the guide in ROUTE 3 (point 5)

ROUTE 3, using the road

1 From Dolwyddelan Castle, leave the car park over the cattle grid and go onto the road, turning right. This is a major road

and quite busy, but you can use a verge for rough walking. As the road crosses the river, look out for cascading waterfalls to your right. After the second road bridge, cross over and choose a minor road going off to the left. On this minor road, a bridge takes you over the railway line and becomes an access drive in woodland edge. You reach a division of drives, and although there is no signage here, take the left-hand option to Bertheos, following the track through the farmyard, turning right and making your way up to a garage affair, where a sign point upwards into a field, left, through a field gate. *Beware low-flying aircraft, although no need to duck.* This track takes you up to a wide double gate with a smaller gate, to the right. Continue up the track. You are looking for a path off right, which is indicated by a marker post by the side of the cart track.

2 Continue along this path, with a glimpse of Dolwyddelan Castle off to the right, past a walkers' sign with a little white man walking, at ground level, and continue down to the river via a gate in the wall ahead, with a ladder stile to the left. Further along go through another gate, which seems reluctant to close, to reach the river which you cross on a stone bridge. A waymark sign on the other side of the river points you off to the right and the path now seems to be taking you in the wrong direction, downstream, crossing another brook coming in from the left. You reach a tarmac access road where you turn left and continue uphill to reach property on the right and make for the field gate ahead. A well-marked grassy track continues upward, winding its leisurely way until it comes to an abrupt and rocky end. You face trees and a stile into the forest. Take a final look at the castle, right, before you plunge into woodland.

3 Follow the forest ride as it contours its way, looking in vain for a footpath off left, as marked on the map, and proceeding to a junction of forest ways. Initially we went left, but this was a false trail, so go right until the forest track reaches a gate and beyond the main road, where you turn left. *Unfortunately you now have a steep and lengthy walk along the side of a busy road, with traffic hurtling down at high speed.*

4 Once you reach the top of the Crimea Pass there is nothing for it but a plunge down the same main road (the A470) into Blaenau Ffestiniog. *Grit your teeth and off you go. You pass the very interesting Slate Caverns, on your left, so if you think you have time for a diversion, dive in. You may not be passing these parts all that often. There is also a ZIP wire.* Carrying on into town, pass a war memorial on your right and make for a significant roundabout, festooned with lamps, where you leave the main road and branch off right. If you have come by bus or train, make your way to this point.

5 **ALL ROUTES JOIN HERE** Cross the railway bridge (*interestingly Blaenau Ffestiniog does not have a bank or a petrol station, but it does have two railway lines!*). You are now on the A496 on its way to Porthmadog but leave it almost immediately. Cross the road on the bend and take the next left, Benar Road. Descend some steps, on the left hand side and up a slope and take the next left into Ffordd Towyn, Towyn Road and walk the full length of the road towards a park-like area where you turn sharp right into Dorvil Road, following this street until it runs out. Look out on the left for a waymark on a post. The footpath you want is between the driveway to a house, left and a yew tree, right. There is a kissing gate and the path descends beyond into a delightful valley, close to the sound of Afon Bowydd on your left. *You have left the built-up area behind you now and the true walk in the countryside lies ahead.*

6 A path comes up from the left, a waymark on the right, and a delightful prospect ahead, in high summer flush with buddleia, rose bay willow herb, ragwort. *I am assured that the fabulous sunny day we had for this walk is not typical of Blaenau Ffestiniog, which has a high rainfall count. I hope you have a similar day's walking along what is now part of the Snowdonia Slate Trail – this 85 mile trek is now open.* A gate across the path, ponies, and a discreet sewage works on the left are features en route. The footpath ends at a ladder stile which you use to take you onto a concrete access road from the sewage works which has cattle grids and kissing gates as markers of your progress. The concrete road takes a left-hand route uphill to end with a shudder at the main road (the A496 again) where you turn left, under power lines, to follow the road as far as the bridge over the river. Here the road bends sharply to the right where you need to leave it to look out for a footpath going east uphill through countryside again.

7 To the left of the large gate, which may be padlocked, there is a small gate providing access onto the hillside. Follow a path sloping upwards under a prominent sycamore tree. Aim for power lines ahead, crossing a stream on a basic bridge, up through bracken. We stopped for lunch here, where there is a waymark on a power line post, but a better spot can be found higher up. Continue toiling upwards, keeping the fence close on your right, aiming for woodland. The path veers right, still following the wall and the fence. Aim to go under power lines, to reach a stone stile, of the old variety, which is embedded in a stone wall, with a waymark. You are

91

at the top, and this might be a better spot to picnic. The way out of this field, which now slopes away from you, is the bottom left-hand corner where there is a kissing gate, and a waymark. You cross the minor road to a kissing gate and waymark on the far side into another field, which you cross, aiming for the ash tree to an exit point with a waymark. You now need to cross another minor road to a gated entry into a field, with a waymark on a post.

8 *You now enter a fascinating section where you need to cross the rushing Afon Dwyryd, but more of that anon.* First of all keep the stone wall to your right, following a track well-marked by animals to a footbridge, an ash tree and continue up the other side, through black sheep on our visit, making for a field corner with a power line junction box on a pole. Go through a gate in the corner. You are now in a lane, a cart track really. Go straight on through the kissing gate, the lane continuing with a wall on each side. This delightful lane reaches another galvanised kissing gate*, on the right.

You can now hear the unmistakeable sound of the rampaging river. *Here we intended to continue to the river and cross it, according to the map. However, if you do go to the far end of the lane, which is worth it if only for the possible glimpse of a kingfisher, you will discover, as we did, that the bridge is no longer there, perhaps swept away some time ago. We were left with a choice here. You could go left here into woodland. There is certainly a path (on the map, at least) which will take you to possibly another crossing point higher up stream. There is even a fallen tree over the river which might provide a way of crossing to the other side, but then there was no guarantee of a path. So we decided to go back up the lane to the galvanised kissing gate.* Beyond the gate, descend through bracken, under power lines and follow a very pleasant footpath in the same direction as the river. You come to a gate allowing you to pass into old woodland, descending to a stile. The path continues to wind its way above the river through woodland and what look like long-legged whinberries. Rocky steps help your descent to a sort of platform area with a wobbly wooden footbridge pointing in the direction you want to go. *From here a quick look at the river over to your left is worth a*

Castle Dolwyddelan **1**

Roman Bridge Station

Bertheos

A470 **2**

3

Crimea Pass

4

A470

Blaenau Tunnel

Gloddfa Ganol Slate Mine

Llechwedd Slate Mines

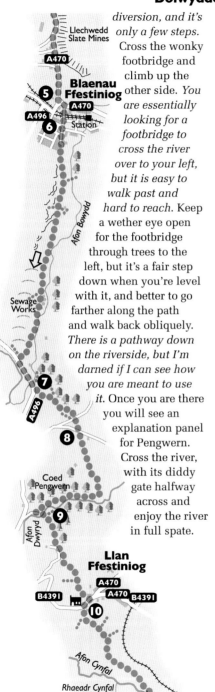

diversion, and it's only a few steps. Cross the wonky footbridge and climb up the other side. *You are essentially looking for a footbridge to cross the river over to your left, but it is easy to walk past and hard to reach.* Keep a wether eye open for the footbridge through trees to the left, but it's a fair step down when you're level with it, and better to go farther along the path and walk back obliquely. *There is a pathway down on the riverside, but I'm darned if I can see how you are meant to use it.* Once you are there you will see an explanation panel for Pengwern. Cross the river, with its diddy gate halfway across and enjoy the river in full spate.

9 *From here it's all uphill to the village of Llan Ffestiniog.* Up the other side you will come to a kissing gate, the pathway taking you round the edge of a field between a fence and a wall up to woodland, with a stone wall on the left. Keep going left and uphill. As you get to the top, branch off to a gate onto a stony track, with a waymark, and come out into a field. Carry on up the field, rightish, towards an old house. Continue up and reach a new wooden gate by the house. There is another gate beyond, a waymark, and a sign which says, 'Shut This Gate', which being good walkers, you do. The track keeps close to a field edge near to ponies, with a laurel hedge on the right. Just before you get to the top there's a path going off to the right, via a stile. This path takes you to a gate, still steeply upwards, until you come to a gate. Continue upwards to reach a stile. Go up the hill to a gate, go through and turn right onto a minor road, as you enter the village of Llan Ffestiniog. At the end of this section turn sharp left along a street, a row of houses to the right. This road will take you up to the centre of the village and the church.

10 Keeping the church on your right, go down the hill on the main road, looking out for a footpath shortly on your left, with a sign directing you to the waterfall, and this is the one to take. You are now in a small field, moving downhill, (*you, not the field*) to a gate, which leads into a larger field. You come to a parting of the ways now, and need to take the footpath off to the left, again directing you to the waterfall. Through a gate you go, to follow a distinct path down the field, making for electricity poles, where the path goes left. Under some trees there is a gate, and beyond, in woodland now, a footpath over a stream. The path goes, upwards for a while, to a kissing gate, continuing with a wall on the left. *You are now making for the waterfall on*

93

the river Cynfal, but note that if you want to see the waterfall the path which you need to follow takes you to a bridge over the river and **not** to the waterfall. You come to a weighted gate. Go through and turn right along to another gate and a sign. You will reach a gate on the access to the nature reserve, and this is where you will need to turn right if you want to visit the waterfall. *Such a spectacular diversion may depend on how much time and energy you have left in your walking day.* However, in order to continue to the bridge, keep left and plunge down through woodland to reach this crossing over the river.

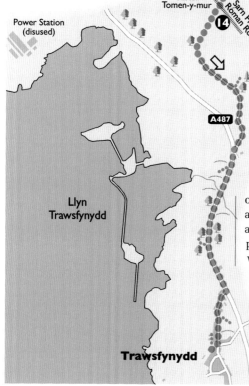

You now have a long climb (over 100 metres) up to your objective, Castell Tomen-y-mur, and at this late stage in the afternoon you need to gird your loins. After the footbridge you meet a walkers' crossroads, where you need to go ahead, and, inevitably, uphill to a stile and enter a large field, with eventually a ruin on your left and another stile. Turn right here onto a minor road, and immediately go off left through a gate. You are now on a bridle path, a mixture of stone and tarmac, with another ruin to the right. You come to a section where the path is signposted off to the left through a very boggy, marshy corner of the field. To traverse this it's better to go ahead, as if to a building and a somewhat redundant and empty information board, so that you can approach the left corner of the field via two sides of a triangle. At the end of the wall, on your right, you will reach the exit point. There is a waymark on a post here, directing you up to a stone shack, with a corrugated roof. Continue uphill to a bridge which carried the former railway line and you pass underneath via a stile. Over the wobbly stile you come out from under the bridge onto a track, turn left and go up with fences on two sides to another kissing gate, into a somewhat featureless field Continue in the same direction making for trees, your objective being a road, the A470. A pylon ahead is a good guide. Cross the field, aiming for a point apparently left of the pylon and as you approach the road you will see footpath signs. Aim for the ladder stile, cross, turn right and follow the line of chain link fencing on your right to another waymark. Turn left here to make the short drop onto the road.

12 Cross the road to find a waymark on a post on the other side, and repeat the process, turning left to follow more chain link fencing then find a waymark and a ladder stile taking you, rightish, onto moorland. *You have to make your own way now.* Go uphill, aiming to the left of the pylon. Once past the pylon, look out for a waymark directing you ever upwards, gradually moving away from the rudimentary stone wall on your right. Persevering upwards you will come to a derelict building a waymark and a ladder stile, which is virtually the top of the climb. Just look back the way you have come and admire the view, all the way back to Blaenau Ffestiniog. Ahead you can now see Llyn Trawsfynnyd and the ghostly outline of the decommissioned nuclear power station. Keep the slate wall to your left as you descend to a gate in the corner and habitation, Sychnant. Once through the gate, keep the building to your right and carry on up the dusty access road. You approach a new house. You need to follow the track off to the right, keeping the building on your left *The OS map here is unclear, and we went well off course the first time, looking in vain for a way through the wood.* What you need to do at this point is follow the track with the house on your left for about 200 yards, and just before the track goes to the right look for a way of getting over the fence to your left. This basic 'stile' consists of two stones with wood across and white flashing on the posts. Walk through woodland and come out over a stile onto a minor road. You have reached the site of the Roman Amphitheatre, and an explanatory information panel.

13 Tomen-y-mur covers an extensive area. Over to the right you will see a large mound, and this is the Norman Motte built on the site of a Roman fort. Go through the gate and follow the path towards the site. You reach a post*, with a waymark, turn right and make for the large mound ahead. There is another information panel along here. Although there is not a lot to see here, use your imagination and you might be able to visualise Roman legions, Norman invaders and others who have settled here on Tomen-y-Mur. Climb the motte for a good view before retracing your steps. When you get back to the original post*, carry straight on to the ladder stile ahead. Once over the stile turn right and go through the gate on your right and continue down the field, close to the fence on your right. Aim for the pylon ahead, and you will reach a gate. Once through, keep the wall on your right and go down the track, which is also a stream, to a footbridge with a wooden rail to the gate beyond.

14 Now continue along the track to pass under power lines, a pylon to your right. Ahead you will see the Lake and the mountains which you will be negotiating on the next leg of your journey to Harlech. Keep close to the wall on your right and find a waymark on a post, always a comforting sight, to join a more stony track. The path bends round more to the left, with a stone wall on the right, to a gate across the track. Finally you reach the field corner and a gate, taking you into scrub woodland. Cross a stream, check the waymark on a post with garish purple hat, and continue downhill picking up a stone wall on your right into something of a gully. You will come out onto a titchy road, where you turn right and go over the bridge which once covered a railway line. Follow this road down to the A487 main road where you turn left. You have less than a mile of road walking and can pick up a cycle track part way before you turn off into the village. If you are looking for a bus stop go right into Trawsfynydd to the Cross Foxes Inn and you have completed a challenging day's walking.

18 CASTELL TOMEN-Y-MUR (TRAWSFYNYDD) to HARLECH CASTLE

Castell Tomen-y-Mur

Chosen by the Romans in the 1st century as a stopping point on a military road complete with fort, bath house and amphitheatre, the site was later occupied by the Normans, who built a motte & bailey fortification, the mound being the most prominent survivor in this desolate location.

A walk in the wild from the heart of the Snowdonia National Park to the stirring might of Harlech Castle high above the sea.

Distance: 11 miles
Gradient: Steep climbs
Terrain: Uneven, rocky at times, marshy, rough grassland
Level: Strenuous

If you are walking the Castles Trail in a continuous journey, you will have probably

ended the previous day's walking in the village of Trawsfynydd, and these notes pick up the trail from there.

If you are completing this section of the trail in one day, you will probably want to be based in Harlech and reach Trawsfynydd by bus. Catch the Porthmadog bus from the main road by the railway station. In Porthmadog the Aberystwyth bus leaves from Australia (yes, that's right, Australia). Allow at least 6 hours for this walk, which is often bereft of signs, at times wet and marshy underfoot with rough, deceptive terrain in parts – watch out for ankle- twisting moments. As is often the case terrain and gradients determine the length of time needed, as much as distance. Mist and rain may make the path difficult to pick out, but we were blessed with fine weather and privileged to enjoy the wonderful views on this wild, perhaps neglected route. And note, there are few traces of habitation on the way between Trawsfynydd and Harlech, so stock up.

A good starting point is the statue to the renowned soldier poet, Hedd Wynn, *who was born in Trawsfynydd and killed in the battle of Passchendaele in 1917.* In the village there are also a free car park, hostel, and public conveniences. Go down past the chapel along the road marked Ty Gwyn and turn right into Cefn Gwyn opposite the Cross Foxes hotel. After the Snooker Club the road turns right by the school and becomes narrower, still tarmaced, before coming to an end. *Do not take the path off to the left, nor the tempting path ahead, which leads to the war memorial, but look for a footpath off to the right.* Go through the gate with a walkers' sign and follow a track, walled on both sides. Further along this track, discover a gate on the left which will take you into a field. You are now heading for the reservoir. Make for an electricity pole. As you approach the reservoir you will see in front of you a long footbridge. Very long, in fact. Go through a gate onto the footbridge. Views over to the right include the brooding decommissioned nuclear power station. Leave the footbridge via another gate and walk along between fence posts to a road, which is also a designated cycleway, where you turn right.

2 You now have a mile or so of untroubled road walking, giving you the best chance of the day to build up a head of steam, so press on. Follow the road.

Where it divides take the tarmac road to the left to reach a farm, Tyndrain. Continue with the road as it veers left and slightly uphill. The road soon bends sharply and you pass through a gate. Continue along the road, keeping a sharp lookout for a footpath sign off to the left by the side of an electricity pole. You leave the road here and enter somewhat amorphous territory. Follow a moist, nay soggy, path to a former farm, Wern-fach, approached by a splendid single piece of slate over a stream to form a kind of footbridge, then over a ladder stile, looking out for a walkers' sign on a post. The path divides here, by the way, so make sure you take the right-hand path, aiming for a distant building ahead, Wern – cyfrdwy. You should be able to see the gable end of this house. But first a ladder stile appears ahead, to be crossed, another focal point in this marsh. You might find a ground-level footbridge over a stream with a waymark, reassuring you of the route, so over the ladder stile you go to another ladder-stile, continuing through boggy landscape (*and this was in dry weather!*) You have now reached Wern-cyfrdwy, which seems to be kitted out as a bunkhouse. Looking back as you leave, you will see signs of a former life, a water wheel.

3 You are now searching to pick up a route the other side of the building and journey on in a north-west direction. Your first objective is a gate to be reached over rough ground. *This next section is even more featureless than the previous one*, and your main guide is going to be a wall to your right which you will now follow, not always close, all the way up to the crags. *In rain or mist this section of the walk could be quite difficult.* You pass what proves to be the last tree, a defiant hawthorn by the wall. Keeping the wall to your right in view should be your main preoccupation, although at one stage it changes into a fence before reverting to a wall. *This is uphill work, gradually getting steeper as you approach the summit.* Another wall comes in from the left with a ladder stile helping you over. A chance now to look back at wonderful views of the valley and distant mountains. But to the task. The path, if path there be, leaves the wall at one stage and there follows a free-for-all as you scramble over rocks ever upwards. At least marshy ground gives way to heather, bilberries and boulders as you see another wall coming in from the right to join 'our' wall on its other side. Soon this marker wall decides to shoot up the mountain to your right, where you say goodbye to it. Keep climbing in the same direction as before, with craggy scree to your right. You are now near the top of your climb and enter a kind of gully, or shallow ravine, with land sloping down left and right. Cross a stream to keep the running water on your left as you continue up to face a buttress-like feature in stone. Go left here, to discover a ladder stile over the wall. From this vantage point you can see the sea!

you will see Llyn Cwm Bychan down below, your next objective. On your descent you will reach a stone wall, with a helpful ladder stile, as you continue towards the Llyn. You are now more or less level with the head of the lake as you come to another wall and a rudimentary stone stile over it, turning to follow the wall close on your left to a wall corner. Go through a gap and, in the next field, cross on the diagonal towards the lake. You're getting nearer to the lake but never reach it. There's a whole myriad of walls here, but keep the main wall to your left, getting close to the trees. You now need to find a path going upwards (*yes, upwards*) off to the right. This path is not easy to see, but it is there and will take you up to the skyline.

5 You come out on top, now with your back to the lake, and the path levels out with land sloping towards you on both sides. As you descend you will see a wall ahead leading your eye onwards towards a building, your next objective, Cwm-mawr. *I have to say we found the next section quite difficult to negotiate, but hope you will benefit from our pioneering work, though the ground underfoot will be no different for you! Just as soggy. Or soggier.*

4 Now for the descent. *A good place for lunch here, by the way, out of the wind, before making your way to the valley below.* The downward track has more of a discernible path than the way up, though rocky. Eventually the path leaves the scree to your right. Ahead, if visibility is good,

6 A flight of natural stone steps takes you down to a ladder stile over the wall crossing your path. Once over, clip the next field, right, to find a stone stile over the wall to your right. You are now making for habitation ahead through a boggy field. After this swampy trudge you will see a wall coming in from the right. Make towards the deserted building ahead through a patch of bracken. Carry on to a gate through a wall, a rushing stream over to your left. Cross delightful subsidiary streams as you approach the house, which you will skirt to the left of the building. You have reached Cwm-mawr. *There follows half a mile of concentrated orienteering.*

7 The direction to take is still north-west, but there is no indication of the start of a path. If you go a little way down the drive to Cwm-mawr you may see the semblance of a path, though on

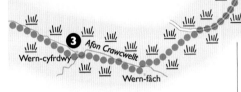

the other hand you may just have to go for it. You need to cross a marshy small field towards a crumbling wall. There is a gap in this wall. Pick up a path the other side walking through gorse where you should find a ladder stile to help you over the wall ahead. Once in the next featureless field you need to walk uphill, rightish, aiming for a five-barred gate in the corner of a projecting field which you can't see yet. But lo! it appears, and you reach it. Turn sharp left here, changing direction to south-west. There is the trace of a path, so walk up to the next ladder stile by the side of a gate.

8 From this point you are basically following the contours of the hill which slopes down from the right, to reach a field corner as yet invisible. We dropped too far to the left, so the answer is to try and maintain height as you progress round the hill through bracken. *There does not seem*

to be a recognizable path. If your luck holds you will reach this obscure corner of a field at a junction of two stone walls, one coming up from your left and another coming down from the right. And a ladder stile. Once over the stile turn sharp right and almost immediately sharp right again over another ladder stile to gain access into a field, which, oddly, seems to be outside the designated Snowdonia National Park. *I don't know what the field has done to deserve this.* However, over you go.

9 You now follow an uphill route describing an arc, and discover this field is in fact two fields, as you pass through an interesting old-fashioned metal gate in the wall at the top of the hill. Continue your arc-like route in the next field. Pass between two rocky structures, making for an exit via a ladder stile almost at the field corner on the left. *You will be pleased to know you have completed your climbing for today.*

10 Once on the other side you find a clear track with a good surface to walk on which will now take you down to the road. This track keeps a wall to the left, and is easy to follow, which is a relief after the featureless climb before. The vista ahead begins to open up, wonderfully. You reach a gate across the track which you

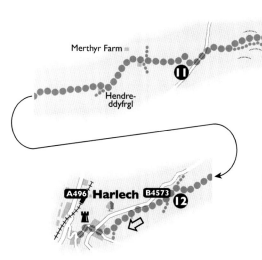

negotiate to reach the metalled road where you turn left. Follow the road looking out shortly for a footpath, signed, off to the right which will take you to Merthyr Farm.

11 From the road the designated footpath now takes a circuitous route across the field, presumably to take in the, now deserted, house in the far right. Your line of direction from the road will be to make for another splendid old-fashioned gate in the stone wall ahead. This section offers breathtaking views of the estuary, backed by mountains, and the whole of the Lleyn Peninsula to your left, so I hope visibility is good for you too to take this in. After the old-fashioned gate you will find yourself in an odd-shaped field. Go downhill towards a copse, walking to the right of the tress, down into a narrow strip of meadow, with trees on the left and fence on the right. Here you will find, at the bottom, on the left, a gate taking you into Merthyr Farm. You need to go through the farmyard, passing close to the buildings and out the other side through a gate,

taking you into a camping area. Continue up through a gap in a stout stone wall to reach another gate. Go through, hugging the contours, making for Hendre. This is the house over to your left, and here you need to change direction and descend sharply to the right, between the electricity poles. There is in fact a marker post with a yellow top to it, halfway down the field, leading to an exit point in the far left-hand corner, where you will find a gate and a track. At the end of the track you come to a ruin, on the left and a gate on the right which gives access to a narrow path and a yellow-hatted marker post, inviting you to take the sharp corner. Round the corner look for the next yellow marker which is downhill by the side of a gap in the wall coming in at right angles, downhill and leftish. From that gate descend the next field on the diagonal, rocky underfoot, making for woodland.

12 You enter managed woodland with a superb old sycamore standing sentinel and just past that a wooden stile leading into Woodland Trust land, Coed Llechwedd. Walk along a fairly level path. Lovely views of the estuary, sparkling with light, to be followed with a remarkable view of Harlech Castle seen through the trees, backlit by the dying sun. Descend steeply through woodland to reach a junction, and go left, slightly uphill. When you come to a fork, bear right, continuing along this access path to reach the cemetery, on the left and a chapel on the right, where you turn sharp right, and right again onto a road. And there is Harlech castle.

19 HARLECH CASTLE to CRICCIETH CASTLE

Harlech Castle

Four round towers of this impressive 13th Century castle built for Edward I dominate the skyline high above the coast. It is now a World Heritage Site.

An exhilarating coastal path tracing the edges of a renowned estuary, as you walk between two ancient castles by the sea.

Distance: 15 miles
Gradient: On the level
Terrain: On established coastal paths mostly, with some road work
Level: Moderate

There is a walk from Harlech to Criccieth comprehensively covered by the Wales Coast Path, well signed throughout.

However, as constituted, this path follows a much longer route, owing to the recent closure of the bridge over Afon Dwrfyd. Now the bridge has been repaired, it is possible to re-route the path from Harlech to Criccieth without having to take the long inland diversion via Maentwrog. Nevertheless, even if you follow the Coast Path without the long inland stretch, the distance from one castle to the other using this method is over 18 miles. To shorten this distance, which might prove a foot too far, I have taken a more direct route, in some cases losing sections, such as the Portmeirion loop, which you may want to incorporate, if you feel you can tackle the extra miles. The route given here is 15 miles, still a challenging target, though mostly on the flat. Depending on your speed, stamina and tea breaks, allow 7 hours or even 8 hours to be on the safe side.

If you are walking just the one leg of the Castles Trail, it's possible to be based in Criccieth or Harlech to complete this section. You will then have a chance to explore the area, including the castle, on a non-walking day. Criccieth castle is open from March to October, 10.00 to 17.00. Admission charges apply. If based in Criccieth theoretically you could catch the 07.38 train to Harlech, walk back to Criccieth and take in the castle before it closes. Just about. Alternatively catch the 09.48 train to Harlech. To reach Harlech castle from the station, which is quite close, take the steep road upwards, possibly the steepest climb of your day. Harlech Castle is open throughout the year, typically 09.30 to 17.00 in the summer and 10.00 to 16.00 in the winter. There are admission charges. Do not linger, as you have a long day's walking ahead. You would probably not be able to visit the interiors of both castles and

complete the walk in a single day. If based in Harlech, the last train back from Criccieth is 20.40. Times based on the 2016 timetable. All the same I would

recommend a Criccieth base and complete the train journey first, to minimise the likelihood of delays and cancellations, and the dreaded possibility of having to rush the walk in its final stages just to catch a train.

Leave the splendid frontage of Harlech Castle by passing under the modern walkway approach, to find a path downwards out of the car park. This tarmac path swings round close to the Visitor Centre, above and to your right, before joining a narrow, steep road, where you turn left, downhill. Splendid views ahead. Ignore the footpath sign to your right. Just as you think this road can't possibly get any steeper, it does. Carry on to the bottom and join a level road, by Woodlands Caravan Park, turn right and follow the pavement. Cross over to the lefthand pavement by the primary school. After the school you run out of pavement so follow the narrow road. Look back at the castle, excellent in profile, before the road ends. Here you turn sharp left, cross the railway line, with care, (*no bridge*) then turn right, following the footpath sign. There follows a long pleasant walk of more than a mile through pasture.

2 At first the path keeps close to the railway line, which is on your right, but look out for a significant change of direction. When you reach a wooden footbridge, the path strikes off at a 30° turn to the left along the semblance of a dyke. You are making for a field corner as yet out of view, close to a field protruding from the left. You find the stile in the corner, the first of many as you keep a straight course, always with the ditch and stream flowing in your direction on your left. Cross a track. Further on, the deep ditch and stream start to change direction, rightish, and here there is a footbridge of sorts, so cross over to the other side. There has been some reconstruction work here, with a new field created. You ought to be able to continue to walk along by the side of the ditch (now on your right) , but there is no stile, and you will have to clamber over the fence as best you can to keep up with the stream to the next field corner. Go through the gate there, keeping the stream and ditch on your right until you reach a footbridge and gateway. *Do not go over the bridge.* Instead turn sharp left and cut across the field towards the busy road. Cross over onto the hectic A496, and turn right.

3 There is no pavement here, and the road is narrow and thick with traffic. Just as you approach the village of Ynys, turn left, thankfully, just before the 30 mph limit, onto a minor, quieter road, which winds its way upwards. *You may encounter a variety of creatures on today's walk, particularly the birds on the estuary, but be prepared here for a llama and a peacock.* As you reach the brow of the hill, with a house on the left, look out for a footpath going off to the right, over a stile to a kissing gate and rough grass beyond. Once in this field go down hill and left-ish, past an electricity pole, making for the stream at the bottom. There is a kissing gate here and a footbridge over the stream into the next field. Bear

left, slightly uphill, crossing the field on the diagonal, with a wall coming in on your right. Make for the gap between the wall and gorse, past a fallen oak. You are now on more of a recognizable track which will take you to a proper road, where you turn left at the footpath sign. Follow the road up to the walled church. Just as you approach the walled church go through a gate on your right where you now join the Wales Coast Path, complete with signs.

4 Once through the gate by the church wall you will find yourself in a field. Go down towards a white-hatted post, with superb views of mountains and estuary ahead. When you reach the kissing gate by this post, don't go through, but keep on downhill, with the stone wall on your left. Good views of Portmeirion over to the left. Descend through a gate into the next field, keeping the wall on your left. At the next gateway saunter through and keep the field boundary now on your right, while travelling in the same direction as before. The path curves round and you go down some surprising steps into a walled lane. You soon reach a field gate and beyond that a road. Turn right on the road towards buildings. *There is a notice here warning you of the time of high tide, although this should not affect you if you keep to the path.*

5 After the cottage turn sharp left and go through a gate onto a raised embankment, or dyke which will now be your route for the next mile or so. After a while change direction, left, by crossing over an isolated and striking footbridge onto another dyke, bearing left along it. Continue now on the right hand side of the dyke. It's tempting to think you would be better off on the other side of the dyke, but stay on the right-hand side until the end.

6 Here you reach a gate, re-cross the railway line, *again with care*, no bridge, and on the other side you need to go, perversely up a hill only to go back down again. At the top of the hill there is a house. Keep well to the left of the house and find a path which you take to return to estuary level. There is now another house on the right-hand side, so follow the boundary round to a gate and beyond that a tarmac driveway which brings you to the main road. Here you turn left. *Roadwork ahead.*

7 Keeping to the pavement on the right-hand side you will reach the spanking new road (and railway) bridge taking you to Penrhyndeudraeth. The Wales Coast Path goes off to the right to make its diversion via Maentwrog, but we carry on over the bridge. There follows a dull but necessary stretch of road walking. As you approach the town you will be directed to the right just opposite the railway station, to find the fleshpots of Penrhyndeudraeth, but it is just as easy to go straight on, up the hill, along a road with no pavements. At the top of the road you rejoin the main A487 and bear left towards Porthmadog. You merge with the Wales Coast Path at Penrhyndeudraeth, though when you reach Minffordd you again part company. *The Coast Path goes off left to Portmeirion, but unless you want to follow this diversion*, turn sharp right just by the Portmeirion sign. This will take you off the main road, down over the railway line to a quieter road. Turn left here and follow this road to The Cob.

8 There are two paths over The Cob. The leeward walkway has views of mudflats and tidal marshes, the seaward side provides a prospect of the estuary and the sea. The Cob is almost a mile long and you walk close to the railway line and road, but mercifully on your own dedicated path. As you come into Porthmadog you are greeted by the friendly hoots of railway engines at the terminus of the Ffestiniog and the Welsh Highland Railways. A useful café, with shop and toilets on your left, will give you some respite after the stern road walking you have just completed.

9 Turn sharp left after the bridge to follow the edge of the harbour. Cut the corner here and make for a roadway, with a sign for the Wales Coast Path taking you round the harbour over to the left, with a high wall to your right. Glance over to the left to see Cei Ballast, the man-made island, and follow the road.

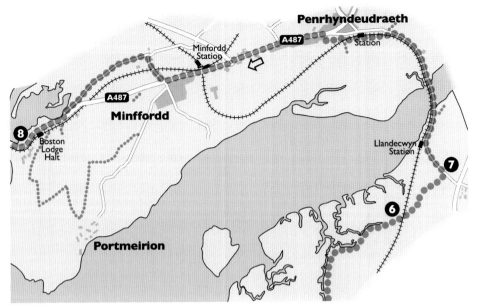

Don't get swept along by the black railings as you need to follow a sign taking you off up and away from harbour level. You reach some houses before going down the other side via steps to the promenade of Borth-y-Gest, as it rounds the tidy bay. Walk along by the seafront, (*public toilets on the right*) but leave the car park area and go up onto the road and into Pen y Banc Nature Reserve. Wonderful views of the estuary. Where the path divides do not take the path down to the beach but continue up slatted steps. The path then turns into a triangle formation, so once again take the upward slatted path under trees to reach a more substantial path, where you turn left, following the Coast Path signs. The Coast Path will take you down to the beach and Black Rock Sands, but there is an alternative. Follow the track you are on, with houses backing off to the left. When you come to a kind of crossroads and a foot-level slate bridge, leave the Coast path and go off right up through a gate into the shrubbery of Windy Ridge turning left onto another tarmac path and eventually through a pretty spacious caravan park. The roadway starts to descend to join a bigger road, where you turn left on the pavement.

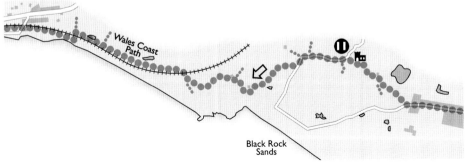

10 There follows an unremitting straight stretch of roadway, relieved by the existence of a shop, where you can stock up on refreshment, before you come to the end of habitation. Still, you can make good progress at the end of the day. After the last house turn off right, through a car turning area onto a caravan site. Here there is a footpath over a stream taking you onto a grassy area. Make for the house on the hill ahead using white-topped posts. An uphill track veers round, right, up to buildings. Here you will notice a gate off to your left taking you into a field. Go through here, but keep close to the field edge on your right as you walk upwards. Skirt the fields on the way up to the old church, turning sharp left at one point, and follow the wall round. Fantastic views of the estuary in the late afternoon sunshine (*hopefully*) as you reach the church via a kissing gate, on your right, which takes you into the graveyard. Two kissing gates, in fact. Go through the graveyard to St Michael's church and out again via the car park to a gate and a road turning left.

11 Continue along the road, downhill, to locate a track at a point where the Coast path comes up from Black Rock Sands. Go off to the right on the side of a hill and follow the signs. This will take you down to the railway line. Cross over the track, as before, to pick up a path which will take you beside the railway all the way into Criccieth. You need to re-cross the railway line one more time before you reach the promenade. As you come into the town your path takes you close to the castle, and, if you are looking for your car at the railway station, that is just a little farther on.

20 CRICCIETH CASTLE to CAERNARFON CASTLE

From the coastal defence of Criccieth, follow a mysterious river, penetrate unexplored wetlands, and track an old railway line to reach the fabulous Menai Straits and the last and perhaps most magnificent castle on your journey, Caernarfon.

STAGE ONE:
CRICCIETH to PENYGROES

Distance: 15 miles
Terrain: From coastal and riverside path through sticky marshland (!) to finish on minor roads and a discrete cycleway
Gradient: Mostly on the level, with no climbs.
Rating: Apart from the bog, easy

To complete this section in one day, catch the A1 bus from Penygroes to Criccieth and walk back along the route given below.

1 from the centre of Criccieth (Café Cwrt is an excellent place to begin) and make for the sea. Cross the railway line and bear right. At the road junction, with its sign to the castle, turn right into Castle Street and continue uphill along this narrow road. To visit the castle look out for the entrance on the left (*payment required*). Castle Street becomes Marine Terrace where you pick up a tarmac path along the front. This becomes a sandy path, the Wales Coast Path now, with the billowing sea on your left. The path decides to venture more onto the beach before straying back among the dunes. You find yourself walking alongside the river on the left-hand side, as it joins the sea, and the river becomes a constant

Criccieth Castle

Built by Llywelyn on the site of a Celtic hillfort, this Welsh coastal castle was occupied and remodelled by Edward I. The occupants were later besieged and the buildings were destroyed by Owain Glyndŵr in the 1400-1415 uprising.

companion now for several miles. Follow the Wales Coast Path, well signed, through a gate to a second kissing gate where it changes direction. Take a sharp right turn here and walk inland.

2 Follow the stone wall on your right, with the sea at your back, until you cross the railway line again. *Look both ways, and listen!* The track beyond the railway veers round, giving a prospect of several blasted oaks on the right, as you approach a house and a gate, with a wall on your right. Follow this wall round to discover steps enabling you to climb over into the grounds of the house, before following the drive round, past models of sheep. You have reached Aberkin. Follow the access road all the way to the main road where you cross, with care, and say goodbye to the Wales Coast Path which goes off to the left. Instead, continue straight ahead, through a gate onto a leafy pathway. This track brings you out onto a road, and if you have time to visit the Lloyd George Museum turn right here. This is Llanystumdwy. Otherwise go straight on, keeping the turbulent river on your left and pursue the road up to the Prime Minister's grave. *The former prime Minister, of course.*

3 Where houses end, go left into the wood, visit the grave and descend via stone steps to follow the path by the river for a couple of miles – a really enjoyable stretch of walking under trees. Look out for foot-catching roots and head-catching branches as you pass through a series of gates. At one gate you seem to be directed down to follow a wet route closer to the river, but if you maintain height and follow the footprints you will find a more congenial way through scrubland and field before rejoining the original path. The river cascades constantly over to the left – a delightful walk, this. You reach a waymark on a post directing you away from the river, so turn sharp right and keep the stone wall on your left as you climb upwards to pass through an archway in the said stone wall. This brings you out onto a minor road where you turn left and continue past habitation, under power lines and bends out to join the B5411 road where you turn right by the letter box.

Afon Dwyfach

Cefn-uchaf Guest House

B4411

6

7

5

Afon Dwyfor

Tyddyn-cethin

B4411

4

Trefan

Afon Dwyfor

3

🏛 **Llanystumdwy**

A497

Aberkin

2

Llyn Coastal Path

1

A497

Criccieth

Marine Terrace

4 Just past the house look out for an access road on your left enabling you to leave the B road and enter a caravan park, Tyddyn Cethin, even though there is no walker sign as you leave the road *It's perhaps worth mentioning that you are now entering a section of the walk which is poorly signed and, later on, poorly maintained. So, after a pleasant stroll from Criccieth you now enter a period of difficult navigation.* Follow the access road, past caravans, to the main house area, advancing between buildings and out the other side. A large gate indicates you are about to enter an unsupervised play area, where you will find a path between trees and low, dilapidated stone walls. The play area is off to the left, but follow the cart track, rightish, which comes to a rather muddy and abrupt end. You need to get back to the river, which has disappeared somewhat over to your left. So, at the end of the lane, keep left, close to a stone wall and pass under power lines. As you traverse the field you will find you can get back on track, literally, and walk more closely to the river again. Cross a tributary to a kissing gate and enter another field. Power lines are now on the right. The map suggests the path goes rightish here,

under said power lines, but as the main aim is to cross the river you will find it easier to reach the bridge by staying close to the river. Sure enough you reach the bridge. Go through a gate and cross.

5 *Navigation over the next section is **very difficult** and the terrain is equally so. The map suggests that the public right of way continues through this next 'field' more or less in the same direction as the power lines. However this is not really a field so much as a marsh, and we found that the way to master this section is to tramp round the bog rather than through it, as follows:* Keep close to the river which is now on your right and use the security of the river bank to keep out of the marsh. *This means you are not following the direction of the alleged path, but it is a viable alternative.* Follow the river bank into a wood, First World War style, and continue beyond, using the river on your right as a guide. Eventually you will reach a fence across your path coming down from the left to the river. Change direction now, go left, and use the fence as a guide on your right to negotiate the side of the alleged 'field', making now for the pylon, of blessed memory. The hedge/fence on your right brings you to a demoralised boundary stone wall crossing your route. There is a gate in the boundary hedge to your right here, which is a useful marker, and if you persevere upwards at this point, with the boundary wall to your right, you appear to be travelling along the remains of a track, with the semblance of stone walls on both sides, so labour on upwards towards the power lines, and you will reach, surprise, surprise, a stile. In the corner. You are back on track. And once over the stile

Ynys Farm

Afon Dwyfach

A487

Llecheiddior-Uchaf

8 **Bryncir**

Melin Llecheiddior

you find yourself on a much better-defined walled track under giant power lines. And that is the way to do it.

6 When you come to the top of the track there is a gate and a weary stile to the right, where you follow another stone wall-lined broad track, as it makes off, right, for habitation, Cefn-uchaf, shielded by a field gate. Go through a couple of gates belonging to this guest house, take the access road down to the main road where you will be delighted to discover a finger post pointing the way you have come telling you that, believe it or not, this is a public footpath. *At this point we tried to negotiate a similarly overgrown 'footpath', marked on the map, which we discovered by taking the road right. There is a hidden waymark on a post here, but our previous experience led us to abandon this idea and return to the Guest House.* So, when you reach the road, turn left and walk along the minor road.

Penygroes

B4418

A487

⇧

Burnt Mound

7 Go to the end of this minor road until you reach a more significant B 4411 road and at the junction turn right to join in. This is much busier, and as there is no pavement, keep your wits about you. Follow this B road for a mile and a half, taking the second left minor road, back over the river. The road bears left at the house Melin Llecheiddior before turning right at the fork. As you continue along this minor road to the top of a hill, look out for a sign off to the right, marked Llecheiddior Uchaf. This starts off as a road but begins to lose status, being labelled 'unsuitable for motor vehicles', passes through a farm and becomes a concrete strip snaking downhill to cross the river again on the other side. You have now reached Bryncir. This is where you will pick up the old railway line, now a cycle track, all the way to Penygroes. *This is your last chance of the day for a cup of tea or an ice cream. To find the Garden Centre Café go through to the main road, turn right and a couple of hundred yards down on the right there you will find it.*

8 Retrace your steps to the start of the cycle route to Penygroes. *I wish I could offer you comfort underfoot, but this being a cycle track it's 6 miles of tarmac. However it is traffic free (apart from bikes), gently rising and falling, befitting old steam trains, and, after earlier painful experiences, distinctly easy to navigate. Perhaps you could set up story-telling sessions with your travelling companions, or sing a few rousing marching songs to while away the two hours of steady walking.* As you approach Penygroes, the first exit point is a roundabout, but continue along the cycleway to the next exit point, right, cross over the main road and make your way into the town and your waiting car.

STAGE TWO:
PENYGROES to CAERNARFON

Distance: 15 miles
Terrain: Mostly cycleway and minor roads
Gradient: Flat
Grade: Easy

Leave your car on the quayside next to Caernarfon Castle, and catch the bus to Penygroes.

Dinas Dinlle

Hillfort

Llandwrog Ffrwd **11**

Harp East Lodge **10**

12

Groeslon

been following. Pass East Lodge on the left, before reaching another main road, which you need to cross with care, again picking up the continuation of the minor road more or less opposite.

11 Amble down this minor road looking out for a lane leading off, just where the road takes a sharp right-hand bend. *A visual cue is a curious sign next to the one banning lorries, which suggests you should also look out for low-flying instruments, spacecraft perhaps. A new one on me.* Go through the delightful village of Ffrwd along the narrow lane. You can understand why lorries are not

9 Walk out from Penygroes along Snowdon Street, following the direction sign to Lon Eifion, making for the sound of the busy main road. You reach a bridge spanning the road, and on the other side find the cycleway, Lon Eifion, created out of the old railway line. Turn right and walk along Lon Eifion. You can make good progress along this broad cycleway, with trees on either side, eventually the Inigo Jones Slate Museum and tempting café appearing on the right. The path decides to cross over the busy main road, to your right, via a bridge, before reaching the village of Groeslon. A field gate crosses your path, with a walkers' gate to the left enabling you to reach a road, where you turn left.

10 Keep to the pavement on the left-hand side of the road, making for a roundabout on the main road. Negotiate the roundabout, aiming for a minor road ahead which continues in the direction you have

welcome. The sea makes a welcome appearance. Next in line is another delightful village, Llandwrog, and here you turn right to keep the church also on your right. Pass the Harp Hotel on the left to a road junction where you continue ahead, following the signs to Dian Dinlle. *Mountains on the Lleyn Peninsula to your left come impressively into view.* When you reach a T-junction, turn right, now picking up the Wales Coast Path, which will be a steady companion on your way to Caernarfon.

A487

LON EIFION **A487**

Penygroes

9

Snowdon St

111

12 Follow the road all the way round now to reach the seafront. It is possible to climb up to the iron age hillfort using a footpath here next to the café. There is no through route to the site, so if you are interested in viewing the iron age fortification, go up and down the same way. Return to the seafront and the promenade and walk northwards, the sea breaking in on the left. This is a good moment, mid-morning, for a cup of coffee in The Coffee Shop, over to your right. At one point there is a severe case of landslip, and you have to negotiate your way round on a temporary path. *Erosion is quite a problem here. Even the hillfort has been partially undermined by the greedy sea. Over to the right the land seems very low-lying. You might see light aircraft coming in off the sea, making for Caernarfon Airport. Not only low lying, low flying.* You come to the end of the promenade, or seafront walk and need to turn sharp right along the minor road, keeping the aircraft complex on your left. Do look out for aircraft, though these are not jets, as this is a low-key airport, and site of the Air Ambulance service. You can also visit the Museum, the Helicopter Simulator and another café. Following the road you now face the impressive backdrop

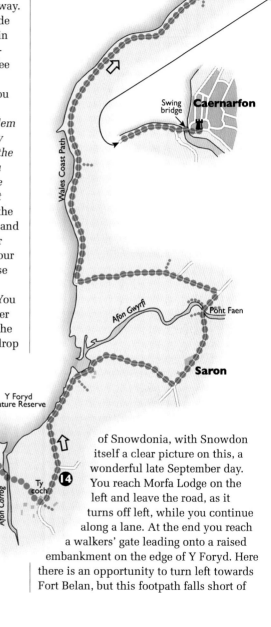

of Snowdonia, with Snowdon itself a clear picture on this, a wonderful late September day. You reach Morfa Lodge on the left and leave the road, as it turns off left, while you continue along a lane. At the end you reach a walkers' gate leading onto a raised embankment on the edge of Y Foryd. Here there is an opportunity to turn left towards Fort Belan, but this footpath falls short of

Caernarfon Castle

Now a World Heritage site, the present impressive Caernarfon Castle was founded on a Norman motte and bailey site and in Welsh hands from 1115 to 1283, before the present building was built, its location identified by Edward I as a royal residence and seat of government.

the Fort itself, and there is no public access to that most interesting of 18th century 'castles'. So leave that visit for another day, and another approach. Instead, once on sweet grassland turn right.

13 A relief to leave tarmac behind now, so walk along the springing turf with mudflats, marsh and wetlands to your left. This is Y Foryd, a nature reserve, and if you are interested in bird life, this is a good opportunity to spend some time looking out for waders, heron, egret and other familiar and less well-known water birds. Continue along the Wales Coast Path, making for a Wales Coast Path sign and a bridge over Afon Carrog. The other side of the river is a muddy walk to property, a field gate and a walkers' gate giving way to another hedge-lined lane. You come out of this complex, referred to as Ty Coch Chatham at a junction with a minor road. Turn left as indicated by the Wales Coast Path sign.

14 Where this road bends off to the right, a waymark indicates you need to go straight ahead along an alternative tarmac road to reach another part of Y Foryd. Anglesey seems quite close now, over the water. Keep to the road, which veers right following the edge of the

wetlands, a useful bird hide on the left. The road now turns distinctly inland, negotiating its way round the mini delta, to meet another, more major but still minor road. Turn left along it. This will take you into the village of Saron and beyond it, along the narrow and twisting road *replete with traffic, beware,* the bridge over the river, Afon Gwyrfi at Pont Faen. Progress uphill and look out for a waymark and minor road going off left, returning to Y Foryd. When you reach Y Foryd, turn right. A good spot to stop for lunch.

15 The route is now fairly plain sailing, an appropriate term as you approach the Menai Straits. Keep to the road, along with other walkers and strollers (*a popular venue, this, so keep a wary eye out for road-hogging motorists*). A church appears, up on the right. Good views of remotely sited Fort Belan, now. There is plenty of activity at a slipway, with boats and divers on the left. There's not much in your way now between you and Caernarfon, and rounding a bend you suddenly see this majestic castle on the quayside ahead. A swing bridge is all that lies between you and the grand fortification. Step over. The trail is complete, and you have walked to all the castles in North Wales, hopefully. *You deserve an ice cream. At least.*

Other long-distance trails available from Kittiwake

The Pilgrim's Way, Mike Stevens
An ancient route across the stunning landsacpe of North Wales, from Basingwerk Abbey to Bardsey Island
134 miles – £9.95 – ISBN 9781908748393

Borth to Strata Florida, Des Marshall
A long distance trail – and a pilgrimage
45 miles – £5.95 – ISBN 9781908748331

Ceredigion Coast Path, Liz Allan
The original coastal path guide, beautifully illustrated
60 miles – £4.95 – ISBN 9781902302676

The Conwy Valley Way, David Berry
The beautiful Conwy Valley from Conwy Bay to Llyn Conwy
102 miles – £8.95 – ISBN 9781902302461

The Dee Way, David Berry
From Prestatyn or Hoylake through Chester and Llangollen to the source near Dduallt mountain
142 miles – £8.95 – ISBN 9781908748218

Glyndŵr's Way National Trail, David Perrott
A fascinating exploration of the best of hidden Montgomeryshire, compiled with the cooperation of the Glyndŵr's Way project officer
135 miles – £9.95 – ISBN 9781908748140

Llŷn Coastal Path, Des Marshall
One of the great British scenic coastal walks
97 miles – £9.95 – ISBN 9781908748263

The Mawddach-Ardudwy Trail, David Berry
Starting from the beautiful Mawwdach estuary and linking the ancient
upland and coastal areas of Ardudwy, linking Barmouth, Dolgellau,
Porthmadog and Harlech
94 miles – £8.95 – ISBN 9781908748102

The Shropshire Way, David Berry
A beautiful walk exploring this recently upgraded trail linking Shrewsbury
with Whitchurch, Oswestry, Ludlow and Little Wenlock
292 miles – £12.95 – ISBN 9781908748317